P9-DDE-360

# Don't Unpack Your Footlocker

HUMOROUS STORIES
OF AN
OVERSEAS BRAT

*Military Family Life — A Kid's View*

Don’t Unpack Your Footlocker

ISBN 978-1-4507-9157-1



dontunpackyourfootlocker@gmail.com

dudleypippin@hotmail.com

Printed in the United States of America

# Don't Unpack Your Footlocker

by

DUDLEY PIPPIN
Author of *Happy Sounds:Humorous Stories of Hearing*

War!

War was no longer just a word. As we came into port, the reality of it hit me.

All that was visible was tons of brick and mortar and twisted steel that had been homes and stores and factories, now heaps of twisted ruins. I glimpsed a little framework or a chimney still standing or a gutted building here and there.

Truly, I now knew there had been a horrific war, wreaking havoc everywhere.

It would be impossible to exaggerate this picture of destruction. Life had disappeared from the scene.

I knew our troops were here to protect the French from further invasion while they tried to rebuild their country, but what I wondered was, "Where in this gigantic wasteland will our family find a place to live?"

# Acknowledgements

With warmest regards I acknowledge the artists who skillfully created the artwork throughout *Don't Unpack Your Footlocker*

Photographer
Charles Flynn

Illustrator
Morgan Mosher

# USS Reuben James
# DD245

Photo from www.navy.mil
USS Reuben James ((DD245) in the Hudson River 29 April 1939
Courtesy: Ted Sloane Collection, Mariners Museum, Newport News, VA
Photo # NH-66333

CHAPTER ONE

# Two Brothers

## The Reuben James

On October 31, 1941 the American destroyer Reuben James was serving as an escort to a British convoy near Iceland. It was a stormy night with very rough seas, which seriously diminished visibility.

Suddenly, the Reuben James was hit forward by a torpedo and her entire bow was blown off. The bow sank immediately. Of the 159 - man crew, only 44 survived.

When the German U-boat skipper, Erich Topp saw the ship, the Reuben James, he thought it was one that the British had obtained from the US. Because of that, he torpedoed it – only afterwards realizing it was an American ship.

He was under strict orders not to torpedo any US ships, and after the mistake, he thought he would forfeit his life when he returned to Germany. However, by that time the United States and Germany were at war and nothing was ever said to him. This tragic error haunted him until his dying days, a couple years ago.

*Story contributed by Air Force Veteran, Harry Cooper www.sharkhunters.com*

# BROTHERS

# LOST AT SEA

US Reuben James
Torpedoed
October 31st, 1941

# The Rocking Chair

# The Rocking Chair

Back and forth. Back and forth they rocked. On and On.

Hour after hour gently rocking back and forth.

Lovingly holding the little one

The Grandmother gazing at the pictures

Rarely taking her eyes from the two framed pictures on the wall

Softly singing lullabies to the small child she held.

*It wasn't until much later I realized the lullabies she sang to me were funeral dirges And the framed pictures on the wall were of her two sons – lost in Reuben James.*

CHAPTER TWO

# Ripples of War

We lived on a little farm of 130 acres in rural Florida; Grandmother, a widow, Mother, recently divorced, Eloise and James, who though they were my aunt and uncle were really more like siblings.

It was a happy, carefree life, and I, though little more than a baby, still enjoyed the few chickens, the cow, and especially the blind pig that was my pet.

And then everything changed!

The USS Reuben James was torpedoed.

Grandmother lost 2 sons, Corbin and Charles.

.Eloise, James and Mother lost 2 brothers.

---

Grandmother—Oma Harris 1896-1974
Mother– Iris Smith 1921-1992
Eloise McDonald 1933-2010
James Harris 1931-1985

Though every effort was made to protect me and shield me from the hurt of it all, yet I knew something had changed. People were always coming over, stopping by, bringing food and gifts.

There was no talk of war or death in my presence; still I knew something was different from before. I didn't know what had happened, but as a child I knew something wasn't right.

A black cloud had come. It wasn't there before. Now it was. I couldn't have explained it; I just could sense it was there.

The ripples of war are far reaching. It might seem the sinking of the Reuben James would have no impact on me. It could appear to be too far removed. Yet it did have an impact. In fact, every day of my life was affected by that tragedy.

Mother had just lost two brothers, one just a little older, the other just a little younger. She was devastated. They had died so young. They'd only had their boyhood. She'd had them such a short time.

The impact of that on her life affected her whole approach to parenting me. She seemed to feel, "Let him be happy; his childhood may be all he has. I was allowed to run free – as I grew older that philosophy never changed.

I went to school, but there was never any pressure to do so; changing schools was not considered important. Homework or studying was never a topic of conversation. She wanted me to enjoy my life.

As time went on, the highlight of our lives was when Uncle Y.J. came. He was stationed close by in Florida, and would often come by. Grandmother's friends always enjoyed being there to see him. It was exciting for me when he came in his sharp navy officer's uniform, and Grandmother was always happy when Y.J. was there.

One day, after grandmother's friends had left, and we were alone, Uncle Y.J. told grandmother that he was really speeding trying to get to her house, when a policeman pulled him over. As the officer came up to the car, he demand, "Let me see your pilot's license." Of course, Y.J. obliged and pulled out his pilot's license. Uncle Y.J. said, "The officer stood there for a long time and looked at me in silence. Then he slowly handed the license back to me and turned and walked away. He got into his squad car and pulled out." The officer had recognized his name; realized Y.J. had just lost two brothers, and could not bring himself to give him a ticket

---

*Y.J. 1916– 1993 Was a brother to Corbin Dyson, and a half brother to Charles Harris. He had hoped to eventually join them on the Reuben James. For reasons known only to the Navy, his reunion with his brothers never came about, and Y.J. got into aviation and was sent to Bermuda.*

*The Japanese attack on Pearl Harbor came while Y.J. was on emergency leave visiting his mother after the loss of his brothers. His Bermuda outfit immediately departed for Pacific duty.*

*Subsequently, Y.J. was accepted for flight training and became a Navy heavy bomber pilot. He spent over 20 years in the Navy before retiring.*

One of my favorite things to do on the farm was to get duck eggs and put them under a setting hen. When they hatched, I dug a hole, put a tub down into it level with the ground, and filled it with water.

When the hen would try to train the ducks to scratch and eat like little chickens, the little ducks would head for the water. She would go crazy trying to get those ducks back; but those little ducks were not trainable. That was great fun.

One evening some one came to the door, and I was quickly hustled out the back door to play. I didn't know why. As a child, I was protected from anything that might disturb me – I wasn't told anything, which is probably why I was the most curious kid around.

So from a vantage spot, I listened. It was a man at the door and I heard them ask him, "What do you want." He answered, "I just want to get my stuff." From something that was said, I realized he was my father. That was the only time I ever saw him until many years later as an adult.

One day a hawk swooped down and grabbed one of my little chicks. He was struggling and pitifully peeping as hard as he could but he was no match for the hawk. I was scared and I didn't know how to help my baby chick. Eloise yelled, "James, get your gun."

James fired. The hawk dropped my little chick. I was furious at that hawk, happy for my chick, but, mostly, I was awed at James, for being able to rescue my little chick when I could only stand there helpless.

---

*Father—Joe Lee Pippin 1913-1993*

The little farm where we lived was very isolated. We could not even see a neighbor, only at night we could sometimes get glimpses of their lights. One night we had an intruder in the house.

Suddenly, grandmother was hurrying me along with Eloise and James out on the front porch. Though nothing was said to purposely frighten me, I could sense the fear in my family.

I could hear someone walking from room to room. Finally, they were gone. We were all safe and the house was safe, but it was a scary time.

Perhaps that's the reason, but not long after that we moved from the little farm in the country to the small village of Bonifay. My grandmother sold the land, but she couldn't get anyone to pay as much as she wanted for the little house.

So, she had the little house torn down, board by board, and moved into town and stacked up in her back yard. I heard people keep asking her why she had all that wood in her back yard. She had piles and piles of wood, even the shingles from the roof.

I got the job of pounding the nails out of the boards. The neighbors didn't have long to wonder. With the wood and the shingles she had a house built on her extra lot next door, and she rented it out for a tidy sum.

Usually when Uncle Y.J. .came, he was all dressed sharp in his navy uniform, and looked great. One day, he did not. Grandmother must have known he was coming because she and her friends were there waiting.

He came in this old, old beat up car, with the doors wired shut and it was smoking like crazy. When he drove up, he pulled himself out of that car through the window, and came inside with grandmother and her friends.

Grandmother got a real kick out of that. He got grandmother laughing and enjoying herself. His coming was always fun for all of us.

# Wedding Bells

Toward the end of my first grade, I came in the house one evening, couldn't find Mother, and asked Grandmother where she was. I learned she had gone to a play at the high school; the high school and my grade school were in the same building, about 5 blocks from the house.

I was very surprised when Grandmother raised no objection to my going and waiting for Mother. Though this was a very small town, it was still much later than I was usually allowed to be out. On reflection, I think Grandmother probably had a purpose.

I waited outside on the school steps. It was probably nearly 10 p.m. when people started streaming out the door; then the stream became a single line, stragglers a few at a time, and eventually Mother with her friend - the two giggling like teenagers. As they spotted me and angled toward me, I had the sudden feeling my life was going to change – and change it did.

CHAPTER THREE

# Country Boy

A short time later, I realized our things were being packed. Mother had married Smitty, and we were moving to the farm with him. Suddenly, I had to leave Grandmother, my aunt and uncle who were really like my siblings, and the security I had always known.

Smitty had not long before returned from serving in the Pacific, and he now had a farm not too many miles away. When we arrived, the large old farmhouse was fragrant from a yard full of beautiful flowering shrubs.

I noticed with relief the black cloud was gone.

There was a smokehouse, a big boiling pot at the side of the house where clothes were laundered – and of course, a three-holer outhouse.

Since Smitty's father and mother lived on the farm, and their large extended family with my many new cousins, was always dropping in, there was no cause to be lonely.

---

*Smitty—Junior Smith   1922-2009*

*Served in three wars, WWII, Korean and Vietnam*

*Smitty's parents—Henry and Martha Smith*

# The Farm

# Cowboy

My grandmother told me since I was going to be a country gentleman, I was going to have my own calf. Her cow had just had a calf, a little bull, and she was going to give him to me. He was my pet, just like a little puppy, since I didn't have a dog. I would hold him by the ear, put my face up to his, and have many a long talk.

After a day at the rodeo it dawned on me, I had my own bull calf. I put my face up to his and told him all about what I had seen at the rodeo – and that we were going to do the same thing.

I jumped on his back, and immediately I went up toward the sky – and then back down toward the ground. That dirt was hard! As I lay flat on my back, I tried first one leg then the other; one arm and then the other. I was surprised I was still all in one piece.

I got that bull calf, grabbed him by the ears, put my face up to his, and explained, "I'm not ever going to ride you again!"

Then I yelled, "But bull dogging, yes!" With that, I grabbed him by the head and tried as hard as I could to twist his head around. He put his hoof down hard, very hard, on my bare foot.

Again, I hit that hard ground as the calf just stood there looking at me. I finally got up, and limping and hobbling over to the calf, I assured him I was not going to ride him or bull dog him again –not ever.

# The Calf

# Sweet Tooth

Mother never did have the heart to punish me; I think the pain of losing her brothers was just still too raw in her memory. Coming home from school one day, I found several of the neighborhood mothers on the front porch with her; the looks they gave me were not friendly.

Mother took me inside and explained we had a problem. "Today, instead of buying your lunch, you went to the store and bought some candy bars." And I said, "That's right."

She continued, "The mothers are furious because their kids copied you and also went to the store and spent their lunch money on candy. They are insisting I punish you." Now, I could see a dim future if all those mothers refused to let their kids play with me.

Something had to be done, so I suggested she do what Grandmother did – use a belt. She exclaimed, "I could never do such a terrible thing." But there was no other way. I was not going to be without friends, so I got a belt, folded it so it would make a lot of noise and do minimal damage, and gave it to her.

The belt made a lot of noise but never did hurt much; however, I started screaming and yelling with all my might. Holding my bottom, I jumped up and down all the way to the front porch, turned around a couple times just to be sure they saw me. I went around the house, crawled under the back porch, and told myself, "That's the most work I've done all day."

# Popcorn

I couldn't get my fill of popcorn. There was a small patch of popcorn on the farm and I was forever after someone to pop some for me. One weekend a lot of the extended family had dropped by, and everyone was just sitting around visiting – everyone except me. I really wanted some popcorn.

I went to each person – one by one – and requested they make me some popcorn but each one responded, "No." I then wanted to know if I could pop some popcorn by myself. "Of course not!"

This was getting me nowhere; so I asked if I could go outside and pop some popcorn; everyone seemed delighted with this solution. It was misting outside and not the best weather in which to pop corn, but the answer came to me. The back porch was raised about 3 feet above the ground, and back under there would be the perfect spot to pop corn. I dug a hole deep enough to build a good fire, laid a piece of metal over the hole, gathered some kindling, started a fire, and put my skillet with popcorn over it.

The smoke began billowing up from the hole; a black cloud of smoke. I heard feet pounding the floor above me, and shouts of, "Not here", "Not here either." Then someone yelled, "Everyone get out!" And I sat calmly under the house, waiting for the corn to pop.

Discovering the source of the smoke, they all started yelling at me. Honesty forced them to admit they had given me permission to pop corn. "But," they protested, "Not under the house!"

Popcorn

# Picking Cotton

One day I realized Smitty wasn’t there. No one had told me he was leaving; just suddenly, I realized he wasn’t there. I asked where he was, and Mother told me he had gone back into service. They needed him and he had gone to South Carolina for re-training.

The timing wasn’t very good. The cotton was ready to pick, and while Mother had had no experience with cotton, she thought we should try to harvest what we could.

So Mother and I picked cotton. We just picked the burr and cotton together and threw it into the bag.

We later learned you are supposed to pull the cotton out of the burr and only put the cotton in the bag. At the cotton gin they said they’d never seen anything like it, but we got some money for it, and it didn’t all go to waste so we felt good about it.

A few weeks after Smitty had left, Mother suddenly informed me that he had been stationed in Colorado and we were leaving immediately to join him. “But my calf? What about my calf? I don’t want to leave my calf.”

But the calf, the farm, family and friends were all left behind as we boarded the train and started out to join Smitty at Fort Carson, near Colorado Springs.

# Head West Young Man

The excitement of riding the train only increased when the Mississippi River came into view. This was not the Mississippi River of my geography book; this was a huge, mighty river – and I was actually traveling high above it. And then, at last – Colorado.

For an active kid, mostly confined to the room on the second floor, there was nothing desirable about the motel we moved into. Then one day when I tried to open the window, the storm window fell, breaking the neon sign beneath it.

That, at least, got me outside to play. I found a friend whose father was American military and his mother was German. Their family had just arrived from Germany.

He could speak a little English so we managed very well together, although he always seemed apprehensive and fearful.

Having just come from my small southern community atmosphere, where everyone knew almost everyone else, I really couldn't understand his fears. As we got to know each other, he seemed to come to realize a friend is a friend, even in a strange country.

Not aware of it then, it wouldn't be long before I, too, would find myself a stranger in another country.

One thing you have to understand about Mother; while Smitty's main concern was to just get a decent roof over our heads, she had a different agenda.

The minute we moved into one place, she would immediately start looking for someplace nicer and more convenient – a better place for our family.

Moving didn't seem to faze her in the least. So, in addition to the moves we had to make because Smitty was transferred, we had many moves in between as Mother searched for a better "nest" for us.

We stayed in this motel for a couple months, then she found a motel with a suite of rooms, then a cottage for a few months, and then she found a very nice, large house for us – but that meant changing neighborhoods, and often changing schools.

CHAPTER FOUR

# Military Kid

## “Sir, Is This OK?”

After a couple of weeks, I decided that since all the other kids were in school, I would go to school, too. I had seen a school, maybe 5 blocks in toward town, so I walked over there and wandered around the school until I found the office, where they directed me to a class.

The kids didn’t like me; I didn't know why. I’d never seen any of them before so why were they so hostile toward me? Actually, the whole atmosphere of the school was hostile.

When the kids learned I was from Florida, it got worse; they asked me questions about the Civil War. I didn’t know anything about the Civil War.

They asked me other questions, too, and when I didn’t know the answers they called me “stupid” and a lot of other names. The teacher didn’t stop them. Every day seemed to get worse and worse.

One day, outside on the playground, a kid came up to me and said, “We’ll protect you on the outside, but they control the inside.” I wondered what he was talking about; I thought and thought until finally I figured it out. I never noticed before, that this boy was (I now know) Hispanic and the ones inside were black. I was the only white person there.

"Sir, Is this OK?"

Then when I went inside, I noticed this kid by the staircase had his eye on me as I went up the steps to go to my classroom. When I got to the top, he demanded, "Get back down here and walk up those steps again the way you should."

I asked him why. "Because I'm in charge of the steps, that's why!"

For a kid who had lived on a farm and in a small town, I resented someone my own age ordering me around like that. Very slowly, I came back down and eyed him, "What am I supposed to do?"

He gestured up, "Take one step at a time, and I am going to watch you like a hawk." I put one foot on the first step and asked him, "Sir, is this okay?" He answered, "Yes."

In slow motion I put the other foot up beside that foot on the step, "Sir is this okay?" Left foot up beside it, "Sir is this okay?" all the way up one long flight of steps to the landing. "Sir, is this okay?"

Then the second flight; one step at a time - almost to the top. By this time we had attracted a crowd of kids and teachers, standing there watching what was going on; wondering what was going to happen.

He bellowed at me, "Don't you skip that last step again."

No one was going to tell me not to skip the last step because I always skip the last step.

I gathered momentum, the crowd moved back, I cleared the step, and just as I hit the landing, a big hand reached out and grabbed me by my left arm, "You are going to the principal's office."

Although I did not know the principal, he seemed to know about me. He welcomed me into his office and explained to me that there was another school close to where I was living. He instructed, "Dudley, tomorrow morning when you wake up, instead of turning right and coming to this school, turn left and go to the stop light.

He emphasized, "Remember do not cross until it says 'walk' because it is across 6 lanes of traffic. Tell them I asked you to come over there."

"When I arrived the next day, they were expecting me, and it turned out to be a great school where everyone was involved in fun activities, including the exciting adventures with the Cub Scout troop I joined.

Of the many schools I've attended, this proved to be one of my favorites

# Boxing Gloves

I made many friends in this school; and as I was wandering around town, I also made friends with some of the kids that went to the other school. Though I thought they had come from Mexico, they emphatically informed me they did not like it at all when people called them Mexican.

I was intrigued with the idea of learning to speak Spanish, however they wouldn't speak Spanish to me because they were determined to learn English.

One day a kid from school, who knew I was friends with the Hispanic kids, approached me to set up a fight between the two groups.

I didn't think this was a good idea, and I balked at doing it, but there was a whole group from the school that was set on it. When I talked with the other group they were all for it too.

Everyone was excited about having a big bang. The anticipation was very high in our school and also in the Hispanic neighborhood.

About this time, I noticed a man following me and watching me. I wasn't totally sure why, but I kept my eye on him.

I was really concerned about the upcoming fight; too many of the kids might get hurt and they were all my friends.

A few days later I was at the home of the kid who had first approached me, and asked him what he thought about turning this fight into a boxing match.

# Boxing Gloves

He had some boxing gloves, so after he thought about it a bit, he agreed, "Why not?" He talked with his guys, who also went along with it, "Yeah, that's okay."

As I started to leave his house, I saw the same man who had been following me, at a distance. I asked the kid if he knew who the man was. "Of course, that's the assistant principal at our school."

The next task was to get the Hispanic kids to agree to change the fight to a boxing match; but I was finally able to persuade them. A date was set, and everyone was eager to duke it out.

I was to be the referee. That was a laugh since I didn't know the first thing about refereeing boxing, having never even boxed; but that was the way they all insisted it had to be.

When the big day came, I took a stick and drew a square in the grassless lot chosen for the fray, as I set up some rules for the crowd of kids that wanted to fight, or just wanted to watch the fight.

Then out of the corner of my eye I saw the assistant principal, trying to be unobserved up the street a ways; but he wasn't coming any closer so I didn't let it bother me.

The boys were all there ready to go. The chosen first fighters were about to get their gloves on and go to it.

Suddenly, we were descended upon by parents; Hispanic parents, white parents, lots of parents; more arriving by the minute. We all scattered – and that was the last I ever heard about boxing or fighting, and I continued to be friends with both groups.

# Hobo Camp

One of the places we lived while in Colorado was in a small town just outside of Colorado Springs, called Fountain.

Though at least a half mile from our home, the music and commotion from the Hobo camp at the large freight train terminal there proved an irresistible magnet to the boys in my neighborhood.

We would sneak up and watch them from a safe distance as they sang to their musical instruments, yelled, and danced around.

This entertainment could go on for hours.

One night we had sneaked up quite close, and when they finally stopped, we then started yelling and singing and dancing, imitating them.

When they angrily began yelling and swinging in our direction, we decided caution was the better part of valor and took off.

# Leaving the Traps

In Colorado, the last place we lived was in a summer cottage by the *Garden of the Gods*. It was my playground and I loved it. It was wonderful.

The owner of the summer cottages had a son about my age and we became very good friends; climbing the red rocks and hiking in the area.

As the weather began to get cool, his father told him he could go with him to do some trapping in the area.

The traps were expensive, but eventually he let my friend set the traps by himself, and as I went along with him, he taught me how to set the traps.

One day, for whatever reason, he didn't come along, and asked me if I would set the traps for him. I was ecstatic.

Each trap was meticulously hidden so it couldn't be seen by the animals; only the bait was showing.

It took a long time because there were many traps and I wanted to do a great job so I would get great results.

The next day I could concentrate very little on my school work; I was so eager to get home and check those traps. I was confident of a good bounty.

The bus stopped and let me off. I was running pell-mell for the cottage before I noticed the cottage was empty, the family was in the car with the back door open.

I was being encouraged, "Dudley hurry and get in. We're moving."

Distressed, I tried to explain to them about the traps. They shrugged their shoulders, palms up. When we had to go; we had to go.

I again tried to explain, "You don't understand; they don't know where the traps are." There was nothing to be done. We had to go.

Smitty was being shipped overseas to Korea and he wanted to get us back to Florida and settled before he left. There was no time. So, I got in the car, closed the door, and we were off to Florida.

I worried for years about those traps. I wonder to this day if he ever found his traps.

# Monkey See, Monkey Do

The little town that I had so reluctantly left when Mother married and we moved to the farm with Smitty, no longer held any appeal for me. We didn't live with grandmother; we were way across town in a neighborhood where there were no kids.

It seemed lonely without Smitty, and we were, to put it frankly, restless.

I spent a lot of time going to movies, watching westerns, where the good guys always catch the bad guys. One of the things they did which I admired was climb through the second story window onto the roof, jump down from the roof onto their horse, and ride away. They did this in many movies.

One day I was sitting in a tree thinking about the movies I'd seen, and my bike was leaning against the tree. It hit me, "If the cowboys can jump on their horse and ride away, so can I."

Without thinking, I dropped down and landed solid on the seat of the bike. It wasn't like the movies.

I didn't just pedal away. Instead the bicycle began to move, tipping sideways away from the tree, and I fell over and landed again – hard.

I lay there for a long time, and finally I thought, "Monkey see, monkey do." This monkey didn't do that trick again, ever.

Mounting the Bike

# Smitty Wounded

Then several months after he left for Korea, the news came that we had always known was a possibility, and always hoped we would never receive.

Smitty had been wounded!

He had been moved out of Korea to a military hospital. It was a tense time as we waited for word of his condition.

Once he started to recover, and we knew he was going to be okay, we realized he was actually safer now than he had been before.

We moved to Hartford, Alabama because when Smitty had gradually recuperated, he was sent back to the states and stationed near Hartford at Fort Rucker.

# Snakes, Move Over

There was a Boy Scout troop at the school in Hartford, and since I had had so much fun with the Cub Scouts in Colorado, I decided to join.

It was a very active group, with many events scheduled which kept us busy, but what I was most looking forward to was the camping trip.

The big day came. We spent the night in tents, and I kept the guys awake most of the night, making noise and horsing around.

The next morning a kid came to my tent and said the scout master wanted to see me. So I got up and went out to him. To my surprise, all the kids were up with their swimming trunks on and standing around the swimming area of the creek.

The scout master asked me if I wanted to earn the swimming merit badge. Eagerly I beamed, "Yes, I do."

There was a small diving platform there. He told me, "Jump off there and swim to the end of the pool and you can have your swimming badge."

I climbed up on the platform and looked down into the swim hole; it was full of little snakes – hundreds of them. I thought, "No, way."

So I yelled over at the scout master, "This swim hole is full of snakes" to which he calmly replied, "I know, do you want you're swimming badge?"

I answered, “Yes, but I don’t want to go swimming with snakes.” He again replied, “If you want that badge.” With that I jumped in and swam as hard and fast as I could.

When I reached the other end, the scout master looked at the other guys and announced, “If they didn’t bite Dudley, they won’t bite you.”

Everyone jumped in, the snakes took off, and I had a great time swimming with my friends. The scout master must have known they were harmless.

Swimming With Snakes

CHAPTER FIVE

# Overseas Brat

## Off to France

And then the word came – Smitty was being shipped to France – and this time we could go.

I was going to be an Overseas Brat!

Smitty left, and the date was set for us to follow. Excited, I announced to the teacher and everyone else who would listen, "I'm going to France. I won't be at school any more."

The day came and passed, and we still didn't leave, so I asked Mother what was going on.

She explained that she'd begun getting things together, but not quite fast enough. She hadn't yet sold the car and there were some other problems so she had asked for an extension date.

Now, I'd quit school and was embarrassed to go back, so I just hung around waiting. When I saw the kids from school, they would give me a hard time for not being in school.

Sometimes before when we had moved, I'd wished that my family had given me a little advance notice to say, "Goodbye" and take care of a few things (like the traps). But now I wasn't so sure that "Get in the car, we're moving"

That way there was no worrying about the move, there was no time to dread saying "Goodbye" to my friends, there was no "hurry- up- and -wait" and there was no embarrassment of still hanging around when I was supposed to be long gone. I never could decide which was easier.

Moving was hard - either way. Finally, one of Mother's uncles, who lived close by and owned the saw mill a couple of towns over, found out about our problems. He just bought the car outright, the other problems were solved, and we were about to take off for France

# Shots, Shots, Shots

With the loose ends taken care of only one thing remained - medical clearance.

So we headed to the medical center at Fort Rucker. We waited and waited and waited.

Finally the nurse came in. She explained to me that I needed six different types of shots.

It was a three appointment series; two shots on 3 separate days. Either I got all 6 shots today or I couldn't go to France and be with the family. There was no option.

She told me she would give me 2 shots in one arm and then 2 shots in the other arm; which she did.

She kept watching me to be sure I wasn't passing out. I could barely sit there, "I'm okay, you can keep going." So she gave me the two more shots, one in each arm just above the wrist.

When the ordeal was finally over, I told her, "I'm seeing cotton balls, white balls floating in front of my face." The nurse quickly grabbed my head and shoved it between my knees, almost to the floor. I thought she was breaking my neck.

She held my head down – it seemed like forever. Finally she asked, "Are you still seeing white cotton balls?" "No, I protested, but I think my neck is broken."

# Ship Ahoy

We were off. First we took a plane to Atlanta. That was some frightening ride. The turbulence was terrible, but then the flight on to New York was fun.

We had to take a bus to the army base, where we waited about two weeks before boarding the ship to France.

When the first mealtime came, Mother told me to go down and eat. "Aren't you coming, I asked?"

She answered uncomfortably that she wasn't sure that she could afford to eat all the meals across the ocean; but she had enough money to pay for my meals. I felt so bad.

I didn't know what to do. It was terrible. I packed my pockets full of food from the dining room and brought them back to the cabin. Mother just sat there and looked at me, and then she said she had found out that the food was included. I couldn't believe the relief I felt at that.

The ship, carrying troops and dependents, took 11 days going across the ocean. It was exciting being on a big ship for the first time and I made good use of that time.

I took shortcuts from the basement to the deck, I explored everywhere and everything.

They kept announcing over the speaker that there were certain areas that were off limits to certain groups.

I didn't know what the names of the areas were, and I didn't know what those groups were so I didn't spend a lot of time worrying about it.

However; they kept yelling at me until I decided there were certain areas I really wasn't at all welcome. For the most part, Mother stayed in the cabin. She was expecting my sister and was sick much of the time.

We hit three storms across the Atlantic. The first two I survived pretty well, but the third one I was hanging over the side of the deck much of the storm.

By this time I had made friends with some of the ships crew.

On reflection, it's my guess their real purpose was to try to corral me. One day this officer came up to me and told me I should go up on deck. I told him I didn't want to go up on deck right then.

He explained we were passing the White Cliffs of Dover. I had no interest in the White Cliffs of Dover.

His tone changed, "This is an order. Get up on deck or you will regret it as long as you live."

I got up on deck. The cliffs were beautiful, and I'm glad to this day that I went up on deck and got to see them.

# War's Aftermath

War!

War was no longer just a word. As we came into port, the reality of it hit me.

All that was visible was tons of brick and mortar and twisted steel that had been homes and stores and factories, now heaps of twisted ruins. I glimpsed a little framework or a chimney still standing or a gutted building here and there.

Truly, I now knew there had been a horrific war, wreaking havoc everywhere.

It would be impossible to exaggerate this picture of destruction. Life had disappeared from the scene.

I knew our troops were here to protect the French from further invasion while they tried to rebuild their country, but what I wondered was, "Where in this gigantic wasteland will our family find a place to live?"

I soon discovered the scene at the harbor was not typical of all of Europe. Recovery had already begun.

Clean up was well underway and rebuilding was in process, with most roads cleared, trains coming and going, and lives being rebuilt. Some cities had suffered very little damage, and those areas had been restored.

# War's Aftermath

# Encore

Smitty met us as the ship landed and we were off to Paris by train. We went to eat and since I had been seated at a separate table near Mother and Smitty, he gave me some French money to pay for my food.

He gave me a hundred franc and a fifty franc and a twenty and a ten and a bunch of small stuff. I was loaded.

It seemed like an awful lot of money.

After finishing breakfast, the waiter came by and wanted to be paid. I gave him ten francs. He said, "Encore" and held out his hand. I gave him a twenty franc.

Then he became very emotional and started yelling, "Encore, encore, encore," and held out his hand again.

So at this point, I looked over a Smitty and he was grinning ear to ear. I knew he was having fun at my expense.

Meanwhile the waiter continued to yell, "Encore." Then I gave him a fifty. He was really angry then.

He was busy and didn't want to be bothered. I finally gave him a hundred. I thought a hundred dollar bill for breakfast was way too much.

Finally, Smitty came over and paid him whatever he needed. Actually, I later learned that a hundred dollar bill was only worth about 25 cents so what I had offered him at first was nothing and then more nothing.

It was right then I realized I was no longer in my own familiar country.

Paris! My first experience with round-a-bouts. It was wild. We were going around these circles and no one seemed to ever stop. It was not only cars, but bikes, motor bikes, scooters, busses, you name it.

What a city! I would be back over and over again to enjoy the Eiffel Tower and many of the other wonders of this special city.

# Ambassador, Me?

We were to first live in Royan, France. As we arrived there we could see the masts of destroyed ships that had been sunk still sticking out of the water off the beach. The area had pretty much been missed by the war and we moved into a lovely home.

A few houses were still bombed out and some were already built back. There were a lot of new homes across the street.

Except for my family, at first I was pretty much all by myself. Many of the other military kids lived on base. We didn't because Smitty was involved with incoming ships so we needed to live in towns near ports rather than on base.

We were trying to settle in to this totally new way of life. Everything was new. Everything was different.

There was always security, but no matter what I always knew my family was there. I had always felt this, but had never been so dependent on my nuclear family.

I had come to know that my home was my family. A house was just a place to stay – irrelevant really - sometimes we lived in a rundown hotel; sometimes in a beautiful home like this one.

What was really important was family. That was something that became so ingrained in me during this period of time that it never changed. A house has always been just that – a place for family.

The kids in the neighborhood all came over to visit us. They wanted to be friends with Americans. They didn't seem to care who we were as long as we were Americans.

It was strange that someone wanted to be my friend not because of me but because I was an American. This was all very new to me. I felt like I was just another kid, but I soon realized that I was like an ambassador for my country. Wow!

I admired the optimistic spirit of the French people. The rubble had mostly been cleaned up by the time we got there. They were rebuilding.

I learned so many French didn't want the war and suffered so much from the enemy. All of Europe was hurt from top to bottom; millions died. Probably no family went untouched. I tried to talk with the kids about the war, but they wouldn't talk about it.

They didn't want to talk about it.

# Mayday

Shortly after we moved in, I met a French boy about my age, maybe a couple of years older than me, who lived down the street. He seemed very happy to have me, an American, as his friend. He especially wanted to practice his English on me.

One evening he asked me to go bike riding with him. He told me as we were riding to keep quiet and not to talk. He would do all the talking.

We went up and down the street yelling. We became part of a group of hundreds of people riding bikes and yelling. It seemed strange. I couldn't understand a word.

It did seem a rather hostile climate. Some people made remarks to me that didn't seem friendly, but I couldn't understand a word they said so I didn't say anything. My friend would talk to them and then they seemed okay.

After hours of this, we decided to go to a movie. It was called "The Living Desert". It was in English and had French captions on the bottom. That was the best part of the evening.

The next day the American kids on the bus to school asked me what I had done yesterday, Mayday. I explained I rode my bike with a bunch of French kids and they were yelling and yelling.

The American kids became very angry and explained their tires had been slashed, windows broken, paint splashed on their cars – all kinds of mean stuff. Their families had been barricaded in their houses.

I had taken part in a communist Mayday rally and didn't know it!

We had extra MP's on our bus to school that day. We would stop at blind crossings with narrow streets and the MPs would get out and check to make sure the bus was not going to be ambushed.

Finally when we got to the base, at the entrance they had sand bags and 50 caliber machine guns. At this point, I began to acknowledge it had been a very serious day. It was a communist day and an anti-American day and I suddenly realized how much the communists hated us Americans.

However, most of the French people liked the Americans and were very happy to have us there. The French kids showed great respect because we were Americans. They were excited and exuberant to be with us because their parents had told them the Americans were the ones that had liberated them.

# The Gang

Our home was not too far from downtown Royan so I decided to go downtown to look around. The buildings were close together, side by side. They were mostly three or four stories high and butted right up to the sidewalk.

I was just starting to walk back toward home, minding my own business when a guy reached out from a doorway, grabbed me by the arm with, "I'm taking you up to a meeting upstairs."

I had no choice. He was American, big, no uniform (though I guessed he was military) strong, late teens or early twenties.

We went up a flight of steps into a hotel type setting and on into a room, where 10 or 15 young guys, some my age, some a little older were gathered. Three or four other guys appeared to be leaders. I didn't know anyone there.

The leader, not the guy that had seized me downstairs, talked. He informed us he was from New York; had run a big gang there; had gotten caught, and the judge gave him an alternative – service or jail for a long time. He chose service.

He was now going to set up a gang here the same as he had in New York. He was going to kick it off tomorrow morning.

What he also threatened was, "We do not take 'No' for an answer." He said he had killed a lot of people and no one dared defy him.

He was terrifying. I was scared motionless – petrified. He went on, "You will be here tomorrow morning – right?" Everyone agreed.

He let us go. I got out of there. I felt as if someone was following me. I knew they didn't know where I lived because we'd just moved there. So, I walked the wrong way for a long ways.

Then I turned and walked another way, still the wrong way. I went through alleys – all over – a long, long time. When I was sure no one was following me, I went home.

The next day I spent the whole day in the house. I didn't go out. I didn't go by the window. I just stayed in.

I didn't tell anyone. I never told anyone anything. After that, I stayed away from downtown. I spent most of my time with my friends at the beach.

# By Ambulance

We never knew when we got ready for school what type of military transport would pick us up for the nearly one hour trip to school.

Whatever was available was what we got. One day a military ambulance picked some of us up and we were off to school.

This day they were running a little late. On the way we had to go over a bridge, a very old Eiffel bridge that had cables dangling from the top to the platform.

It was not safe for heavy equipment and the military was not allowed to use the bridge except an ambulance with an emergency.

This day we *were* in an ambulance. The driver didn't want to go all that extra twenty miles to another bridge so he asked me if I'd like to be a patient. I said, "Sure."

The guard and the driver put bandages on me and wrapped me all up as a patient on the bed in the back.

At the bridge toll booth, she stopped us with, "Military isn't allowed" but when she saw me in the back she okayed them to go through.

The driver told me we can't do this very often; otherwise we'll get into trouble.

# Moving Again

It wasn't too long after we arrived in Royan that my sister, Sherry, was born. Mother had to go to the military hospital at La Rochelle, about an hour and a half away.

Soon after the baby was born, I came home one day to find we were all packed and ready to move. I guess we now needed more room.

Then we moved into an older neighborhood that had many more Americans living there.

This home was not too far from a very nice beach where I spent a lot of time swimming and enjoying a lot of American friends as well as French friends.

It was also very close to some nice fishing areas and I was very happy to be able to grab my pole and go fishing whenever I wanted.

# The Eel

One day I had been fishing at the harbor and something kept stealing my bait. I lost my hook, I lost my sinker and the line broke. I just couldn't get him. Finally I used a rock for a weight and put a new hook on and just a little piece of bait right on the end of the hook. I said to myself, "I'm going to catch him this time."

I left the line taut so if anything touched it, I would jerk that hook right into his mouth. And I did. I finally caught him. It was an eel at least 3 feet long.

I was so excited I couldn't wait to get home and show my mother. She was sleeping, lying on her side, very close to the edge of the bed. I held the eel right up to within an inch of her nose.

I was so excited I screamed as loud as I could, "Look what I caught." She opened her eyes and all of a sudden she lifted straight up, right straight up off the bed and landed against the wall beside the bed.

She was screaming and yelling like the world was coming to an end. I'd never seen anything like it. I'd never seen my composed mother like that before.

I told her I was taking it to the kitchen and cleaning it for supper.

She screamed, "No, no, get it out of here. Get it out of here. Get it outside." And she didn't stop screaming until I got outside.

I decided I had better not do that again.

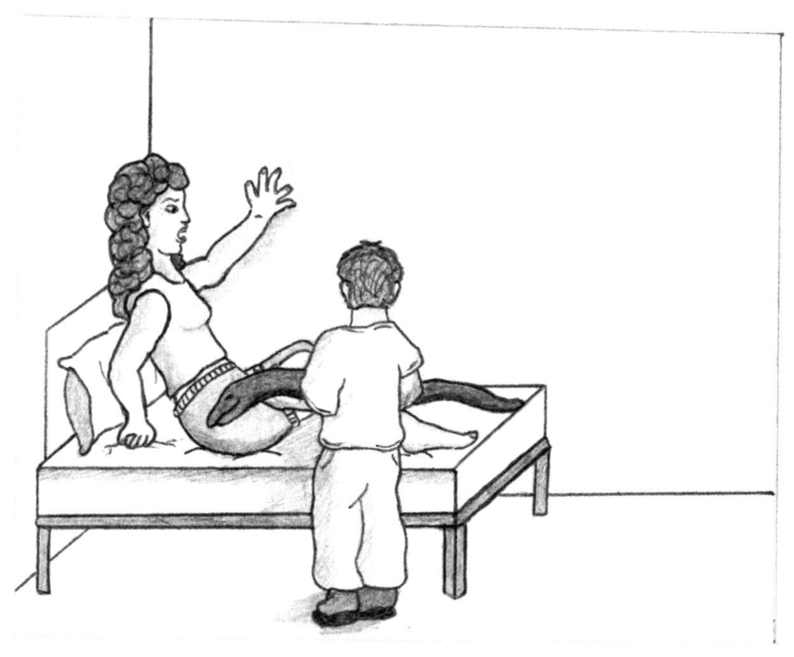

The Eel

# Flying Backwards

Having ridden my bike quite a ways from home, I stopped in a fairly large park just to rest, sitting on my bike watching a group of 15 to 20 French boys on their bikes When they saw me, an American, they came over and talked with me, asking me about America and all the latest trends.

They believed they knew about America because they had been studying the book about Tom Sawyer and Huckleberry Finn on the Mississippi River.

Then they happened to notice my American bike, different from their French bikes, with wide tires and funny handlebars; they laughed and laughed and laughed.

Well, they had had their fun and I thought they'd leave, but they didn't; so I explained to them, "In America we ride our bicycles backwards."

This really set them off: amid less than complimentary comments in broken English, gestures, and shouts of laughter, I jumped on my handlebars and rode backwards, then turned around and rode backwards back to them. They were dumfounded.

Then I continued, "The ones who are really good ride backwards without holding onto the handlebars," This sent them into gales of laughter.

Again, I jumped on the bike, and as it gained momentum going downhill, I held my arms out as though I were flying backwards.

At that, the whole group jumped on their bicycles backwards; the French bikes, with their “goat horn” handlebars made sitting and riding backwards impossible and they ran into each other, flipped over, and all landed on the ground.

Some of the bikes were damaged, and as I rode sadly away, I knew that, so soon after the war, money was hard to come by, and those families had had to sacrifices to buy those bikes. I never saw any of those kids again.

Flying Backwards

# German Bunkers

On the way to the beach and to my friend's house I would go by this German bunker. One day I stopped and opened the door and went inside.

It was quite an experience because I was sure soldiers had been occupying this not too long before. Later I found many more German bunkers which I played in and around.

This was very different from the places I'd played before like the creeks and swamps of Florida and the beautiful Rocky Mountains.

It was a new adventure for me and something I enjoyed doing on my own.

Later I found out that when the French went in to destroy these bunkers they were heavily mined and two of the soldiers died.

They just covered up the bunkers and made a park out of the area, leaving only the top of the bunkers so they would not forget what had happened there.

# School for Babies

One day Mother asked me to take my little sister, Kay, to school.

I protested that she was only 3 ½ years old. At home children didn't start to school until they were 5 or 6 years old. In France she was required to go to school.

The younger American kids went to nearby schools but we older kids had to be bused to high school.

I took her the few blocks down the street to the elementary school.

There were many other kids already there, but the real small ones were all bunched together crying their hearts out.

I thought that, "They'd never be allowed to send babies to school if I had any say about it."

# The Mud Hole

As time went by, I found there were American kids around; I just had to find them. Most of them were my friends but there was one kid down the street that definitely wasn't my best pal.

One day after playing with some friends, I was on my way home. I saw Jack in front of a house. I knew the American girl that lived there. She was one of the girls from school. Her father was an officer.

Jack had a bouquet of flowers in his hand. I yelled, 'Hi' to him. He came back with some sarcastic remark and added, "I'm going on a date with an American girl, something you wouldn't know anything about."

I didn't like his attitude at all, but I did stop and listen to him for awhile.

Then he got really smart, and he made a mistake; he poked me in the chest with his finger. I suggested he grow up. He leaned forward and was about to again poke me in the chest with his finger.

I grabbed his arm and put him on my shoulder like a bag of cotton. I kept turning, whirling around and around and spinning him around and around as I went.

There was a mud hole close by and I let him fly. Flat on his stomach in that mud hole he landed, still holding the flowers.

When he got up he was screaming like a stuck pig, and crying.

Now he wasn't so sarcastic or condescending. His attitude had been rearranged. The flowers were a mess, and he was a muddy, wet mess.

The girl's father came out on the second floor balcony when he heard Jack yelling. He bellowed at me that if he were down there and could get hold of me, he'd use all his military training on me.

That was kind of scary and I took off as hard as I could. Jack never bothered me again.

# Bait and Switch

I have to admit whoever engineered this one was pretty clever. All the kids – French kids – American kids – all had heard about this movie that was coming to town and they all wanted to see it. Everyone was talking about it. It was really talked up.

There were big ads for it everywhere. It was supposed to be a real sexy movie and the kids were real excited because teens could get in; they just needed a permission slip if they were under a certain age.

Finally the day came. There were long lines to get it. Well, I didn't have a note; I couldn't be bothered to get one. I didn't really care. I didn't go to many movies anymore. There was too much sitting and there were many more exciting things I could find to do.

"Well", the kids said to me the next day, "It's a good thing you didn't come." They had been grossed out. I guess it had been a government documentary about sexually transmitted diseases. It was very graphic; it went into the dangers of STDs with distressing detail. The descriptions of conditions went on and on. Apparently they'd had problems at prior showings because there was an ambulance standing by. Most of the kids got sick. Almost no one stayed to the end; they couldn't take it.

I really felt sorry for my friends. They had so looked forward to being allowed into this highly advertised movie, and now they believed, and probably rightly so, that they had been "had".

# We Cook Our Food

Some of my friends heard that two sisters, high school girls, were coming to town for the summer. Their mother and father had just moved here into a beautiful beach house and word was their two daughters would soon follow.

So these two guys and I headed over to their house to see if the girls had come yet and to welcome them.

We got to the house, and as we were just going up the sidewalk, the maid was coming out muttering. She appeared frustrated and confused, shaking her head and as we got closer she waved her arms at us and included us in her muttering – some in French, some in English - “stupid Americans, dumb....dumb.”

We were only able to make out, “We cook our meals before we eat them.”

We didn’t know what to think about this.

Then the mother came to the door and laughed and explained, “Each time we travel to a new country we like to get the favorite dish of the local people and try it, so we went to shop at the nearby market.

There they prepared the dish for us to bring home for dinner. We sat down to eat; we were really trying to eat it and it tasted terrible, really awful.

Then the maid came in and astonished she said, 'In France we cook our snails before we eat them'.

The market had prepared the dish ready to *cook* not ready to *eat*, but not understanding the language very well we didn't get the message."

Well, back to the subject of the daughters.

The mother smiled that the girls had already met French boys and they really wanted to date French boys while they were in France and had the opportunity, so they would be tied up all summer.

We said, "Fine, we just wanted to welcome them."

# Softball, French Style

A short time later I wanted to play softball. So I got a bunch of the neighborhood guys together and invited, "Let's play softball." "Never heard of it," they objected.

I decided to teach them to play softball. I got my ball, bat and gloves and we headed to a nearby field. I showed them how to lay out a softball field. I started explaining to these boys how to play softball.

I went into great detail about the batter, the catcher, and each of the bases – first, second, and third. And, I explained, to get someone out they had to get the ball and touch the base or touch the person before they got to the base.

So finally the time came, and we chose up teams. I thought I did a good job explaining even though I was going through a translator that knew nothing of the game.

The pitcher got up to throw the ball and the batter hit the ball and these soccer players started to play softball. The batter was headed for first; the pitcher got the ball but instead of throwing it to first base he threw the ball and hit the guy in the head.

I again explained, "You don't hit the guy in the head. You hold the ball and touch him. You don't hit the guy." (I later saw this guy take a rock and knock a bird off with one throw). The guy wakes up and doesn't want to play anymore. He wasn't too sure about this game.

So, the game begins to go again. This batter hit the ball and he started running. He got past first and started for second. The guy that caught the ball began chasing the runner and he cut him off from second base so the batter headed for the outfield and then beyond the outfield; the guy with the ball still pursuing him.

This went on for a long time. These were soccer players. They could run forever. Finally, on a hill, he tackled the guy and he held up the ball letting us know he'd touched him so he'd be out. And he hadn't hit him in the head. Then they began their journey back to the ball field.

Meanwhile others had been working at learning the game, and we all decided "not any more today".

Then I did the unthinkable. I took my ball, my bat, and my glove and went home.

This was one of my least successful attempts at public relations.

# Landlady

When I got home the lady that owned the house had returned. She hadn't been there since we moved in because she had been in Vietnam, She lived in one section of the building.

She was with the French military and had just come back.

She started screaming at me because I was an American. She said they had been defeated and it was our fault because we wouldn't come to their rescue. "If you had, we wouldn't have had a problem."

I didn't know anything about it. I didn't know what she was screaming about and blaming me for.

But I now knew more than ever that the world had been at war and was still at war. Now I heard it at school, I read it in the military newspaper, and was constantly reminded that we kids had to be on alert and could be moved out quickly if need arose.

# Helpful?

One day while visiting one of my French friends one of my American schoolmates asked me to come over to his house explaining they were very cold and their furnace wasn't working. Their parents were gone for a week and they really needed some heat.

I asked them why they didn't call the landlord and they replied that they couldn't get hold of him. I admitted I didn't know anything about furnaces but I'd look at it.

It was a furnace that water circulated though – a hot water furnace. The problem was it had no water in it. They had that furnace turned full on and it was red hot.

I explained that we could turn the cold water on and let some go very slowly into the furnace but it would probably take quite awhile because the furnace was so hot the water would have to be added very, very slowly. So we turned on the cold water to allow just a small amount to run in at a time.

Finally there came a little heat. He got all excited and wanted me to turn the water on faster. And then faster. I shook my head, "Only if you take responsibility." He promised he'd take full responsibility. As I turned the water on faster, a big crack developed.

I groaned, "That it. It's wrecked."

I felt really awful about the whole thing and decided right then I'd never pursue a career as a furnace repair man. I moved right after that and never did find out what happened.

# Towel Dressing Room

The beach at Royan was beautiful and I spent a lot of time there. It was a different culture; for one thing the swim wear was very skimpy by American standards. It didn't bother them, so it didn't bother me.

I was fascinated at the way the girls would come to the beach fully dressed; then they'd throw a large towel around themselves and they would change. Street clothes off, and out they would come with a bikini on in almost no time.

And when they were ready to leave the beach, the towel would go back around them, and just like that, bikini off and they were clothed and ready to go with dry street clothes.

I would always say, "Wow!" As a kid I was very impressed.

I had some very good French friends that I enjoyed being with on the beach. They spoke English quite well and we had fun talking, swimming and just hanging out.

One day they brought with them a beautiful French girl. She didn't speak a lot of English, but I could tell they all thought my education was sadly lacking when I admitted I didn't know how to French kiss.

She offered to teach me some day, but alas, I had to move before that day ever came.

# Bicycle Built for Two

I made good friends with a well to do family that lived not too far from my home. After I'd know them for a while, they said they had a bicycle built for two that I could have. It would need only some minor work.

I was so excited. I took it to the repair shop. They gave me a ticket and told me I could pick up the bike the end of the next week. I could hardly wait that whole week. I just wanted to get on that bike and ride it.

The next Monday morning as I got ready to catch the bus for school, Mother had suitcases packed for me to take with me. "We're moving."

I was anguished as I explained that the bike would be repaired by the end of the week. She could only shrug her shoulders with her palms up. When we had to go, we had to go; and I had to leave the bicycle built for two there in the repair shop.

Mother did not know where we were moving but it would be too far for me to come home each night. I would have to live in the dorm on base and come home on weekends.

She cautioned me, "I don't know where we will be, so don't come home until you hear from us."

# Dorm Life

Going to high school in Rochefort was nothing new. I'd been going there all along, getting up at the crack of dawn, taking the long ride to school and being immediately rushed into class.

Then the buses were waiting as soon as we were dismissed to take us for the long ride home. I'd had very little time to even notice much about the base.

Now all that changed. It was like a whole new life.

The dorm buildings were Quonset buildings. There were two boys' dorms: one for 11th and 12th graders, with about a dozen guys, the other for 9th and 10th graders with about 20 guys.

The dorms were open like a barracks but divided with partitions that went nearly to the ceiling, so while they were all open to the hall, there still was a certain amount of privacy.

Each area had room for 2 boys, with a bed, locker, dresser and desk. The two dorms were connected by a building containing bathroom facilities. We boys didn't seem to have problems with the limited facilities, but I guess the girls did.

We had a dorm supervisor. He had a room (actually a small efficiency) but he was in the other building with the younger guys. He also did something else around the school. I never did figure out what that was.

When we left to go to breakfast and then on to school, the dorm had to be clean. Beds had to be made neatly, military style, and all personal stuff had to be put away.

While we were gone to school, French ladies came in to clean. They swept and scrubbed, emptied waste baskets and cleaned the bathroom.

But, anything that was left on the floor or lying around was swept up and thrown away.

## Game Room

The game room was actually connected to the boy's dorm but there was a solid wall that separated the two so there was no entry into the game room from the dorm.

Girls were allowed in the game room. We had a lot of fun there and could go there pretty much any time except assigned times like school time or study time. There were tables for games such as chess and checkers and there was music if anyone wanted to dance.

We spent a lot of time playing ping pong, and it's something I played and enjoyed long after my dorm years.

The Arch

# Base

When we got to the base, we drove up to a guard house and checked in at the gate where there were always at least two military police (MPs).

We then drove through the base and over to the school compound restricted area. There was another smaller guard house with an MP there. The driver checked in with the guard and we walked through the gate into the compound. There was a service area road but normally no vehicles drove into the school area.

The only entrance to the school compound was through that gate and the compound was surrounded by a tall fence, probably 7' high. On top of the fence was a barbed wire extension of about 3 feet angled in a v shape; one side angled in and the other side angled out – virtually impossible to get over.

While the dorms were Quonset buildings, the school was not. It was an old, three story French building which the Germans had occupied when they were in the area. There were about half a dozen classrooms on the first floor, including the nurse's office, and about the same number on the second floor, including the principal's office. I got to know both of these offices very well.

On third floor was the biology lab. We first went to homeroom for roll call, Bible reading, the pledge of allegiance to the flag, and prayer.

# Kids From all Over the World

Many of my school mates were kids from all over the world. This was mostly because troops had married French, German, English, Italian, Russian, Philippine, Japanese, Jamaican; we even one student from Venezuela.

Some of these were children from former marriages, and they were traveling with the military as dependents.

Not all the students in the school were military. There were ambassadors' kids, as well as children of Americans that were in France for a variety of purposes.

There was one thing that had apparently been well established by the time I arrived. There was no discrimination of any kind. I never once heard it brought up. I never felt any kind of undercurrent. And after my Colorado experience, I'm sure I would have. That was probably why I was so keenly aware of it.

There was no difference made between the students. Rank of parents was never brought up and discussed by teachers, staff or others. At least I never heard it. I was not ever aware of it. The teachers overall were very good. Most were young and spent their weekends traveling to different countries

# Salty Prank

Now, while Mother had always allowed me to run free and enjoy myself exploring wherever I pleased, the military had an entirely different approach for students living on base.

The only time students were allowed out of the compound area was to go to the lunch room and the theater.

The lunch room was about a two block walk (we walked right past the French dry dock which is where the Hermione is now being reconstructed).

The snack bar was run by the military but the employees were civilian French. The food was not the American style we were used to, nor was the service the fast pace we were used to.

The food was okay, though; it was somewhat like a short order bar with soup, sandwiches, dessert and a full breakfast of eggs, toast, and meat, or whatever we liked.

There were assigned times we were allowed to go to the lunch room. We had a specific time to be back into the restricted area. We usually went and returned as a group.

The military was not allowed there when the students were there. We were totally separated from them. Anywhere we were; they were not. We were very much cocooned.

Our parents gave us money to pay for our meals for the week. I was usually down to nothing by week's end.

One day someone took the salt shaker and loosened the top on it so when I used it the cap came off and my food was ruined. So I thought I would do the same thing to him and when he next sat down there, he would get his own back.

So on Friday noon, my last meal before going home, I happened to sit at the same table. And I happened to pick up the same salt shaker. And again, my chili was ruined. I was out of money and it would be many, many hours and late at night before I got to eat again.

That was the last time I ever played that prank.

# Where Did You Say Home Was?

So the end of the week came. On Friday I got my suitcases, there were at least three or four of them because I had to take all my clothes home to be washed, and headed out to the buses. There were at least ten or twelve busses and since I wasn't going to the same home, I didn't know which bus to get on.

I had no idea where I was going. What I did know was that I'd been told everyone had to leave the dorm for the weekend – and I hadn't heard anything from my mother. What to do, I didn't know. I just knew I had to leave, and I had to take a bus.

While I was standing there looking at the busses, some one came up to me and asked me my name. When I told him, he instructed me, "Get on bus #22 going to Bordeaux." Bordeaux was in the southern part of France, nearly two hours away.

I questioned, "Where do I get off the bus?" He answered, "You'll go over a large river and when you get across it, count very slowly to 100 and then get off the bus."

That made me nervous.

When I got on the bus, I told the guard (we had drivers and guards) who I was and asked him if he knew where I should get off. He had some idea, but he wasn't sure.

I talked to the kids on the bus to see what they knew. They knew where they lived, but they didn't know where my family lived.

Finally an hour to an hour a half later, almost to Bordeaux, we went over a large river and I started slowly counting and walking toward the front of the bus. Then they stopped while I got my suitcases, which were piled in the back of the bus, and they let me off.

And the bus left.

I didn't know where I was. I didn't know where I was going. Because I had asked as we were riding along, I'd found out where some of the kids lived. I had closely watched when they got off—just in case. No one lived close to here.

I was standing there with all my suitcases. We were within a foot of a very narrow road. The suitcases were almost in the road and huge trucks were whizzing by. I didn't know where any military base was anywhere in the area.

There was a little cluster of houses within feet behind me: just a few isolated buildings huddled together right out in the country. Actually, where they had let me off was in the middle of a vineyard. So I took my suitcases and moved them back into the little space away from the road up by the building.

Hoping I could somehow find my family, I stood there as those trucks were flying by non-stop, my eyes and ears on full alert searching for something; anything.

Then over to my left, about a block away, I saw a movement. There was a huge farmhouse with a big metal gate and a little girl playing in the yard – my sister, Margie!

With great glee, I picked up my suitcases and headed for home.

# Outsmarting the Termites

The old farm house was actually a large French chateau, probably about 300 to 400 years old; made of large quarry stones at least a foot thick. It had at one time been the home of a large vineyard owner. Now they had a new, modern home some distance away.

We had the run of that huge old home, except for the small apartment of the vineyard keeper. He never would talk with me. I never knew why. I tried to talk with him, even tried my limited French but he simply would never talk. Maybe it was because I was a kid, maybe not. I never did figure it out.

I began to explore that old chateau from top to bottom. It had high, high ceilings. I discovered many secret compartments. I had found a bunch of very small old keys and I was investigating to find what they would open.

Nothing was obvious, but when I ran my hand along the old wallpaper, there would be a sudden indentation. Close examination would find a spot that had a slit in the paper and by digging around I would find a small keyhole.

Then I would try my bunch of little keys until I found the right one, and a whole section of the wall turned out to be a door that would swing out and reveal a storage area. It was like a hallway, and all along it at various spots were these small nooks and crannies that these little keys would open.

I was disappointed I found no treasure and no secret tunnel.

One day, while alone in the house, I wanted something to eat. There was a large door that led to the pantry, reaching to the ceiling and very heavy and wide. As I pulled the door back, it hit my foot.

The bottom of the door where my foot had landed sheared off. Where my foot had hit –the size of my shoe –a chunk of wood just cracked off.

This was very frightening for me because I knew if I had broken this huge door it would cost a fortune. I looked inside and the entire inside of the door was full of termites and eaten away.

The outside of the door looked fine, but the inside was honeycombed. I picked up the piece that had fallen out and pushed it back into place, and it held. What a relief! I took off.

There were vineyards with grapes everywhere. I was fascinated by them but I did not want to get involved learning and working with grapes. I had been on the farm, and with the cotton and all, I had kind of had it with any kind of farming.

Besides, I had discovered the base was only about 20 miles down that main road with the military trucks whizzing by, and I could hitchhike there and back. There were all kinds of interesting things to do on base.

# "Please Stay Awake"

The French teacher, Mrs. Massaid, was French. She was determined to teach us proper French.

Boring! Total waste of time! I kept asking her, "Why don't you teach us so we can just talk to the French people." She would always reply, "No, I have to teach you proper French." So I learned kitchen French from the French kids, and could actually communicate quite well by the time I left France.

We sat in class and repeated over and over the lists of words she gave us. Well, anyhow, what with not sleeping too much at night, and the constant drone of the (to me) nonsense syllables the class repeated nonstop, I often fell asleep.

One day the principal came in, came down to where I was sitting, sat in the seat behind me, and kind of tapped me lightly on the shoulder.

He said, "Dudley, I know this is boring, but please just try to stay awake."

The only thing I really remember from that class was that Mrs. Massaid told us she had gone to Britain to take classes to try to improve her English.

She found, to her surprise, that while the French history books always stated the British started all the wars, the English history books stated that all the wars were started by the French!

# Roll With The Punches

This year we had a new counselor. She called a lot of students into her office and I was one of them. She gave me a test where I had to pick out things I liked. Most of the things didn't make any sense. When I finally got through, she told me I was half and half; half scientific and half social; and it was very unusual to be half and half. I told her that was okay. I was sure glad I knew who I was.

Then she exploded her bomb. She was making me repeat 10th grade. I was flabbergasted. I wanted to know why in the world she would want to do that. I had passed all my courses last year. She insisted there was one mandatory course I had to take before I could be in 11th grade, and also she wasn't going to accept a lot of other credits I'd had from the states.

I argued and argued with her. I'd taken all the 10th grade classes and I had passed them. All to no avail! She absolutely was not going to change her mind.

It wasn't until years later at reunions that I discovered she had done this to any number of students.

Normally, I'm not a person who gets angry very easily but I was extremely mad, violently mad when I got back to class.

One of the girls noticed how upset I was and asked me what the matter was. I told her I had to take the tenth grade over again for no real reason.

I made up my mind that this wasn't fair, and I was going to make absolutely no effort to study. I would pass, but just barely. Since I'd taken all the required subjects before, this year was very easy. I signed up for library, soccer, and other fun stuff. I had nothing really to study.

There was another reason this was really awkward. I'd just started living in the dorm as an upper classman. If she put me back in the 10$^{th}$ grade, I would belong with the younger kids. That would be crushingly embarrassing. I just never told anyone, stayed in my dorm, and didn't let on there was anything happening.

There was one more incident. One teacher gave me a "B" for the semester. I had been strictly adhering to the pledge I'd made myself of passing – but barely. A "B" did not fall in that category. I told him I wanted to talk to him after class.

When I asked him why he gave me a "B", he replied, "Because that's what you got." I objected that that was not "B" work I'd been doing and that I aimed to pass, not to get a good grade.

He just sat there for a long time, looking straight ahead as if this is something I will be telling my grandchildren. Finally, he began, "Dudley, I had to grade on the curve, and you fell into the "B" range. That's the way it is."

I told him I guessed I would accept it then.

# The Sky is Falling

Our homeroom teacher, Justus Brown, was really a nice guy and he had told us a little bit about himself. He was a Native American from Oklahoma. I didn't know until later that I was part Cherokee along with my Scottish and English. Anyhow, this teacher had a habit of walking back and forth, back and forth in front of the room.

One day after he had been pacing, he stepped out of the room for a few moments.

While he was out, with a deafening noise, part of the ceiling crashed down right in front there where he always paced. It was a very old building and the hole in the ceiling was about 6' x 20'. Debris was all over his desk and the surrounding area. No one said anything; no one moved.

He'd heard the noise and came in yelling – and when he saw the disaster, he shouted at the top of his lungs, "Who did this? Who did this" The whole class answered him with one voice, "Dudley did it" and pointed to me.

He grabbed me by the arm and thundered, "We are going to the principal's office."

He started to calm down just before we got to the principal's office. He looked me straight in the eye and asked how I did it. I defended myself, "You know there is no way I could have done that."

He stood there pondering for a moment, shook his head and turned to go back to the room muttering, "We'll say no more about it."

# Bumps

One bus we rode to school was the kind that had tires just behind the middle of the bus. Well, the roads were old and had sunk, so when we came to little bridges over creeks and streams, the small bridges were higher than the road.

There was a sharp incline, then the few feet over the bridge, and then right back down again.

When I would see we were coming to a bump, I would get the kids together in the back of the bus and as we went over the bump, we would all jump at the same time.

When we got to school, I asked the driver if the front end came up. He glanced at me and grunted, "Yes, but it came right back down again."

He didn't seem to care so this was one way we had great fun and relieved the boredom of that long ride to school.

# The Eiffel Tower and Flying Buttresses

The Rochefort American High School had only been in existence for a year or so when I arrived so it wasn't tremendously structured. This was great for us as students because we were taken on a lot of field and sports trips, which we loved.

Paris was my favorite and we spent a lot of time in that area. We were allowed to climb the Eiffel Tower - much higher than is allowed now and we could see forever.

The beautiful gardens reflected centuries of careful manicuring. We visited old cathedrals with buttresses and flying buttresses.

We went to Nantes. It's an old city that had once held a Roman garrison. Lions had fought in the old theater, which still remained.

We visited coliseums and castles; we went where the Crusaders had been and enjoyed history with a front row view. No history class could take the place of what we experienced first hand.

# Bag Boy

After hitchhiking to the base and exploring the area a few times, I learned American students worked at the commissary for tips. They called them bag boys. They bagged the stuff and carried it to the cars, and the shoppers gave them tips.

But they had enough bag boys.

I walked around and as I went by the meat department, I saw the guy running it was working by himself. He seemed really busy, so I asked him if he needed any help.

He said, "Yes, I sure could use some." I helped; I packaged meat or anything he asked me to do. And, matter of fact, he came early and worked about an hour before the store opened. So I came early and worked before the store opened. This went on several days.

One day after working about an hour in the meat department, he told me to go on up and pack groceries. When I got up there, they didn't need any bag boys. I told him; he went up and ordered, "I'm half boss here, and he is going to work here as much as he wants to."

So after that, I got to work every day. The others had to take turns; but I got to work every day.

I had to hitchhike there every time – about 20 miles, but there were always guys going to the base so I always got there and home at night.

This was my opportunity to be with Americans other than students. In the small towns where we had lived, Americans were few and far between.

What I enjoyed most about working there in the commissary was I got to meet soldiers. I could mingle freely with them.

When I was in the dorm we met no soldiers or other Americans on base. Here I could listen to the American women as they grocery shopped; as I packed their groceries, and carried them out.

It was an aspect of observing Americans living in France that I was able to get in no other situation. There were all kinds of people. I talked with officers, trainers, maintenance people; everyone.

The entire base, at one time or another, seemed to pass through the doors of the commissary.

On the base was a Polish camp. These were displaced Polish soldiers that had been in France during the war. They were not allowed to go home because the Russians controlled Poland and would not let these soldiers return.

They had no place to go and were living in tents on the base in a section set aside for them. The would buy their groceries at the commissary.

I enjoyed having French friends but it was nice, also, to have American friends. When we lived here, near Bordeaux, I did have one American friend that lived about a mile from me. His family rented space in a huge 16 bedroom house from the French family that owned it. He and I spent time with the kids in that family who were our age.

We got involved in new aspects of French living and culture as we went to their French carnivals and other celebrations together.

# French Underground

One day while working in the commissary, I was sent to get a load of bread from the bakery, which was in a separate building about a half mile from the commissary.

A French civilian employee drove the truck around the base picking up bakery and whatever else was needed. I had worked with him there in the commissary and he knew me.

On the way over to the bakery he pulled between two barracks and stopped and kept his eye on the road that fronted the barracks.

I asked him why we didn't go to the bakery, get the bread and head back to the commissary and work. He didn't say anything; he didn't move either. I kept prodding him, "We have to go." "I really want this job." I was really pressuring him, "Let's get going"

Finally he leaned forward, "A plane will be coming in to this base for a surprise inspection by an American general. It will land in about 5 minutes, and then a car carrying the general will come right in front of us a few minutes later."

We waited. Sure enough, the plane showed up and the general passed by us just as he had predicted.

I realized I had just met a member of the French underground. He was in a tough spot. If he said nothing, I'd be explaining why I was late getting back to work; or he could tell me and hope I'd keep quiet.

I did.

# French Underground

# Principal's Office

It seemed interesting things were always happening in homeroom; nearly every day something came along to break the monotony. I was finishing my homework way in the back of the room when a kid in a nearby seat handed me a funny toy with a cork in the end and a trigger in the middle.

I pointed it toward the wall and pulled the trigger. It emitted a large puff of smoke and a loud noise that echoed through the room. I handed the toy back to the guy who gave it to me.

The same nervous teacher, bellowed "Who did that?" and again, all fingers pointed to me. I was on the way to the principal's office when the teacher stopped and asked where the gun was. He left me in the hallway, waiting. By this time the toy was safely back outside the window cell.

The teacher and the principal, Mr. Dillon, got into a big discussion over the incident that went on quite a while. The teacher considered it almost like a shotgun with real shells; the principal's view; it was nothing, really.

I couldn't find a chair, the only place available was a cabinet, about four feet wide, so I got up there and lay down while they argued.

Finally the principal turned around for me. He saw me on top of the trophy cabinet, and started to talk very softly and carefully, and gently helped me down off the trophy display.

Very calmly he asked me to go back to class and not to let

The teacher stayed with the principal and I started to go to my next class.

As I was walking down the hall, the teacher from the class I should have been in, but obviously wasn't because I was in the principal's office, was coming up the hallway very fast.

She grabbed me by the arm and said sternly, "Dudley we're going to the principal's office."

Just before we got to the principal's office, I asked her why were going to the principal's office. She told me that a cork had been put in the door frame and when she closed the door it had exploded.

I asked her why she thought I did it. She said everyone in the room said I did it.

I grinned, "You're going to look pretty silly if we go in there with that story because during the whole last period that's where I've been – the principal's office!"

# Look to Tomorrow

Homesickness was something that was always there but no one really ever talked about. When we were sitting around talking, after a person had talked for a while, you would know what he was really missing because he would start talking about it; mostly about home.

What kids seemed to miss most was family; older brothers and sisters and other close family, especially grandparents.

Many of the kids were from other countries and they would talk about their home. One guy from Venezuela (I think his father was the ambassador) talked about Venezuela. I felt especially sorry for him. We had each other from the states, but he had no one from Venezuela.

In the Stars and Stripes, (the military newspaper) we read once about a kid from another school, who had gotten so homesick that he had somehow obtained a motor boat, and started out on the ocean for home. He got 50 miles and ran out of gas.

The Stars and Stripes was a source of military news, but also the source of what little bit we could get about what was happening at home.

When a new kid came, we all wanted to talk with him or her to see what was going on at home. What were the latest songs, the latest fads, the latest everything?

Often the teacher would leave the room, "I have to be out fifteen or so minutes and you can talk among yourselves." That would give us a chance to question the newcomer.

One of the hardest things to face was when a couple had formed a very close friendship, and one of the families had to be transferred out.

This happened fairly often. The day after one of the guys had to leave, a bunch of us fellows were headed over to get something to eat.

I noticed the guy's girlfriend was out by the guardhouse. She had her hands up on the fence, gazing over at the gate. She stayed there for a long time.

That day she didn't go eat at all; just stayed by the gate.

After we passed through the gate, and followed the outside of the fence toward the snack bar, I could see her face pressed right up into the wire of the fence, staring over at the gate, devastated .

That is an image that has been burned into my memory.

# Dudley Smith

When you live as interesting a life as I did, the nurse's office becomes almost as familiar as the principal's office.

One day I was in getting some aspirin, and a corporal was manning the nurse's station at the moment (I think he was the military representative there at the school). Anyhow, he started to fill out the report (everything was paper work in the army) and seeing my name was 'Dudley' he immediately asked me if I knew a Dudley Smith.

"No, I don't." He persisted, "I am looking for a Dudley Smith." I shook my head, " No, that's not me, and I don't know any Dudley Smith." He grumbled, "I've been looking for months for a Dudley Smith."

Finally, he wanted to know who my family was. "My stepfather is Junior Smith". With this I saw his eyes light up. He'd put two and two together.

He turned to me and yelled, "That's it, that's it." He then went from happy glee to almost rage. "You have caused me so much grief." I guess his superiors must have really been on his back to find Dudley Smith. I can't say I was ever his favorite person after that.

Months later, when I went for bedding issue, he happened to be the one giving it out. He saw me and made me go to the end of the line. When I finally got back up there, he said, "I'm not giving you any; you've caused me too much grief." I just turned and left. Relenting, he came running after me, "Here we'll give you some."

# Friends and Foes

We moved north to St. Nazaire. The post was small with only 50 to 100 military personnel, and a few were military police. There were several small buildings including a cafeteria where our family sometimes went to eat, a small interdenominational chapel, an infirmary, other military buildings.

This town was different from the other French towns where we had lived. There were many more French communists.

The large shipbuilding area of town was run by the communists. They called it their union and we stayed out of their part of town. It was dangerous and whenever possible we went around it.

Most of the people were pro - American and I was told many times how much they appreciated our coming and helping them when they needed us. That always touched me.

Most of the French kids there welcomed us from the very first day just as they had in the other towns.

This time we netted a very nice house about a block from a beautiful beach. I lived on that beach all summer.

From the beach we could watch the ships coming in , only 50 to 100 yards from where we sat. Most of them were Russian ships, which came in to be serviced, although there were also ships from other countries, as well as our own U.S. ships.

# U.S. Go Home

Communists were easy to spot because they were not friendly. They hated us because we were Americans.

There was one kid whose family was communist who would talk with me and be friendly during the week, but Friday night, after he had gone to his communist meeting, he would throw rocks at me from the cliff.

It was lucky for him they always missed me. My French friends told me to try to just ignore him.

When I first went to St. Nazaire, the high walls around the streets were covered with graffiti saying, "us go home", as well as other rude things against America.

I wrote up some cards "U.S. Go Home" and took them around to the taverns and little stores in the area, explaining that in English "us" really meant them; so those signs really said they, themselves should go home.

If they intended the message to mean for us from the United States to go home, they would need to change them.

I suggested if they were going to paint derogatory signs about us; the least they could do was use proper English. My success rate was small; the signs did not change, but I felt better.

From my work at the commissary, I bought a German shortwave radio that could pick up radio Moscow. It was in English and, of course, it was their propaganda station. I heard about the five year program and the ten year program.

Everything seemed to fail, and everything was the fault of the Americans. However, it was in English and I was intrigued with their thinking.

When I got back to the states, I began listening to Havana. When Castro took over, I might have been listening to an earlier recording of radio Moscow. Same story.

Everything was the fault of the Americans.

U.S. Go Home

# Float, Boat, Float

As in Royan, along the coast there were many German bunkers that I, of course, investigated. I could get into most of them and explore. Now in these bunkers there were also tunnels. I did not go into the tunnels.

There were signs in both French and German that the tunnels had not yet been swept for mines and NOT to go beyond that point; and in this case it seemed wise to heed the warning.

I knew that two or three miles down from the beautiful beach where we swam, was a small beach.

What I didn't know was that right out from it were a number of underwater barricades to prevent enemy ships from landing.

One day I had a small motor boat and I was going slowly along the coast just to see what I could see. It was high tide, and as I turned to go into that beach, the small lighthouse way up on the hill overlooking the sea, started flashing its lights like crazy.

I thought, "That's strange. I've never seen them flashing before. I wonder what's happening."

As I got closer to the beach, the tide started to go out. As the water receded, the top of the barricade became visible.

The problem was. I was stuck on top of it. The boat was about to capsize. There was no one anywhere around. I tried and tried to get off that barricade.

I did everything I could to keep that motor end from going under, because if that back end went under, the boat would sink. I had to keep the boat balanced on top of that barricade and try to figure out what to do.

It was scary.

Now I knew why the lighthouse lights were flashing all those warnings. They were for me. Too late! Finally, a large boat went by out in the water.

I watched it's wake and just as it got to me and washed over the barricade, it lifted the boat, I pushed with my foot with all my might; the boat skimmed the barricade and started to float!

# Don't Unpack Your Footlocker

We always knew we were in France to protect them from an invasion from Russia, and we were talked to about what we would be expected to do if the Russians did invade. We were to be always on the alert.

I was especially aware of this in St Nazaire. If the Russians invaded Hungary and continued on toward France, dependents were going to be evacuated to Spain.

We felt confident our military would slow them down until we got out. One thing was for sure.

Our footlocker was always there; always packed – a survival kit. It contained just the bare essentials: toothbrush, tooth paste, comb, shirts, pants, underwear, jacket, shoes, and maybe whatever few treasurers we could crowd in. The knowledge of that danger always hovered in our minds.

Since we were always moving, and traveled light, there was little room for keepsakes and memorabilia.

For that very reason, when years later, I found Mother had somehow saved my first grade report card, I was touched. I wonder what of her treasures she had to sacrifice to make room.

Maybe she reasoned I'd made the honor roll and that wasn't likely to ever happen again.

# The Tide

The man that lived next door was a Greek colonel that had fought with the communists in the war of '49 in Greece and was exiled to France. He let me use his boat and motor so I could go out fishing.

One morning I was out in the bay, somewhere between a half mile and a mile out. I'd stopped the motor, dropped the anchor, and was fishing when I suddenly realized the tide was going out; and it was going out extremely fast.

I needed to get that motor started and get myself back to shore as quickly as possible. The motor wouldn't start. The anchor wasn't holding. I was being swept out to sea at a frightening pace.

I kept working at that motor, and after about twenty minutes it finally kicked in, but the boat was still headed out to sea and the current was too strong to turn it around. I angled it a little to the left against the current, still being pushed out, but at a much slower pace.

I kept working that boat around, and by the time I finally got it headed back toward shore, I was all of ten miles out.

I got up all the speed I could and finally, just before I ran out of gas, I got close enough to shore I could row the rest of the way in. I spent the rest of the day pulling the boat along the shore until I got it back where it belonged.

That day I learned about tides.

# "Vive les Capitalistes"

On one strip of the coast, there was an area with high cliffs which were very visible to all of the ships coming in. The cliffs were virtually straight up and down, with a flat surface.

I and my friend who was visiting me, thought this would be a perfect place to write a message for the men on those ships.

The Russian ships had bright flashing lights that at night were used to sweep the entire area as they approached the harbor.

Our dilemma was how to get far enough down on the face of those cliffs to paint without falling and killing ourselves. We devised a scheme.

We tied a rope around him and I lowered him over the edge. There was no place for him to get a toe hold and no way to support him.

As he dangled in mid air, he used a wide brush to quickly paint, "*Vive les Capitalistes*" (Long Live the Capitalists), and then yelled to be hauled back up. My arms and back were more than ready to be finished with the ordeal of holding that rope and supporting him.

Early the next morning the Greek man from next door saw me in my yard. He gave me an ultimatum. I had twenty four hours to get that paint off the cliff or I was dead.

It hadn't really required any brilliant detective work. The paint I used was the paint he had left over from painting the boat he sometimes loaned me.

That night we had a re-run - my poor friend dangling on a rope, using a wire brush to scrape off the paint; and me stretching to hold him while he did it.

If we hadn't cleaned that paint off, I'm sure I wouldn't have been dead, but the chance that he wouldn't loan me his boat again was a risk I wasn't willing to take.

# Bicycle Built for Two

When I learned a field trip to the beach at Royan had been planned, I was overjoyed. Hopefully with a little maneuvering, I could get to that repair shop and retrieve my bicycle built for 2 which I had had to leave behind when we moved from Royan.

From the American school at Rochefort to Royan was a little less that an hour's drive, so it was still fairly early in the day when we arrived at Royan.

The driver and the guard were really nice guys and when they heard my story, were willing to drop me and my friend off fairly close to the shop, with the understanding that we would ride the bike to the beach where they were headed.

To my great relief the bike was still there; and both of us mounted the bike and took off for the beach as promised.

The bus was not at the beach, and there were no students in sight. Now what?

This was the largest and most popular beach, but there was the possibility that they had gone to the smaller beach across town; so off we rode the three or four miles across town to that beach. They were not there either; and the trip back again to the big beach was fruitless.

We were in a quandary; but actually the only option was to bike down along the coastline, checking each area as we went.

They had to be at a beach here somewhere.

After biking down the coast until we were nearly exhausted, and getting pretty desperate, far in the distance we spotted a tiny beach - and there sat our bus!

The driver and the guard helped us cram that long bike into the bus aisle; and back at the dorm compound; even though there were not roads for traffic, there was a lot of paved area, and all of us gave that bicycle-built-for-2 a real workout.

# CIA

A young man from the post, who was not much older than me, would every so often come by the house to see me. He didn't want to do anything special, just hang around with me and do whatever I was going to be doing. He said he was in Special Forces. That was very unusual.

Granted, I was the only American high school student in that town, but still military wasn't allowed to associate with students except in their official capacity. But, if he wanted to come with me, he was welcome.

Remember the boat I was using? He was the one that went with me and persuaded the Greek man to let me use it. He knew about the man next door. He is the one who told me all about the Greek man and his situation.

Then, a few weeks later, he brought an older man, probably about 40, someone he knew from base, and wondered if that gentleman could go fishing with me on some weekend.

On the weekend my friend from school was staying over with me, and this older gentleman showed up to go fishing. We went out and tied up at a buoy and fished for awhile.

A Russian ship started coming, and a French airplane kept diving close by taking pictures of the ship all the way into port.

The man slumped over with his head down and pulled his hat down over his face, griping something about not being in the pictures.

As soon as the ship went by and the airplane was gone, he asked if we could come out again the next day. The next morning we three headed out.

We had lead weights on a large string and we dropped them overboard until they hit bottom and then pulled them back up a little.

Not having any luck, my friend swirled the weight meaning to send it far out in the water, and hit this gentleman behind the head. He was moaning and groaning, so I asked my friend not to whirl that weight anymore because it really didn't help catch any fish, and it was dangerous. He agreed.

We fished for a while and caught nothing. So, as my friend started to whirl his weight, I yelled, " No", which caused the man to turn his head sideways and get caught right in the temple.

He was knocked out cold. He fell to the bottom of the boat. At first there was just weak moaning; then more moaning and muttering: "I'm in the middle of the ocean…. CIA … why am I here… couple of idiots …."

So finally after we had helped him up on the boat seat, "I announced, "I've had it. We're going in." On the way in to shore, this gentleman grimly questioned me, "What have you been doing? What have you been up to?"

I protested, "I have been doing nothing. Well, a long time ago, I did buy a pair of jeans at the PX for a French kid. I'm not supposed to do that, but otherwise, 'No."

He told me he didn't know what I was doing, but he sure was getting a lot of reports on me. I had no clue why the CIA would be interested in me.

# "Don't Talk, Don't Move"

One evening a group of French kids invited me to go along with them as they wanted to do something special at midnight. Of course I agreed.

So late at night, I met them on the beach and we proceeded up a steep cliff toward a large tree on the top. Then we climbed over a wall with glass embedded in it.

It was pitch black. I couldn't see a thing. We finally got to the tree; an apple tree.

We were up in the tree eating apples when we heard this noise, and one of the kids told me in broken English, "Don't talk, don't move."

It was then I realized we were in someone's yard and someone was down there. And that someone might have a shotgun. We froze. We waited.

At last we heard this person walking away. We waited some more. When we finally deemed it safe, we got out of there.

Solemnly, I pledged to those kids, "I'm not going to do that again. I can't take it."

# The Fishing Hut

One day I was walking on the shore with one of my French friends, when we met a French fisherman who was a neighbor of my friend. The French gentlemen asked me if I'd like to go fishing with him.

I was really excited. He had a fishing shack. I had seen the shacks all along the shore but had never had the opportunity to go in one before.

There was a huge net on a pulley with a crank down into the water that was pulled up and down. He told me to come back when the tide was coming in.

So, about ten o'clock that night, we sat around in the shack with a few other Frenchmen working the net. The net was at least ten feet square.

They would throw bait in the center of the net and let it down into the water with the crank. When they heard fish feeding they would pull it up and gather in the fish.

Each man took his turn and finally, about 2 o'clock in the morning, it came my turn.

I told him, "No, that is okay," but all the men nodded I should take my turn. When I did, the net came up full of fish – big fish.

This was a very poor neighborhood. They lived in tiny houses; trying to rebuild their lives after the war and struggling to provide for their families. These fish were their only means of support; they really needed these fish.

Yet they insisted on sharing with me, they insisted I take the fish, which I did.

It was really their way of saying, "Thank you" to an American for our forces coming to help them.

It made me proud and thankful that America had come.

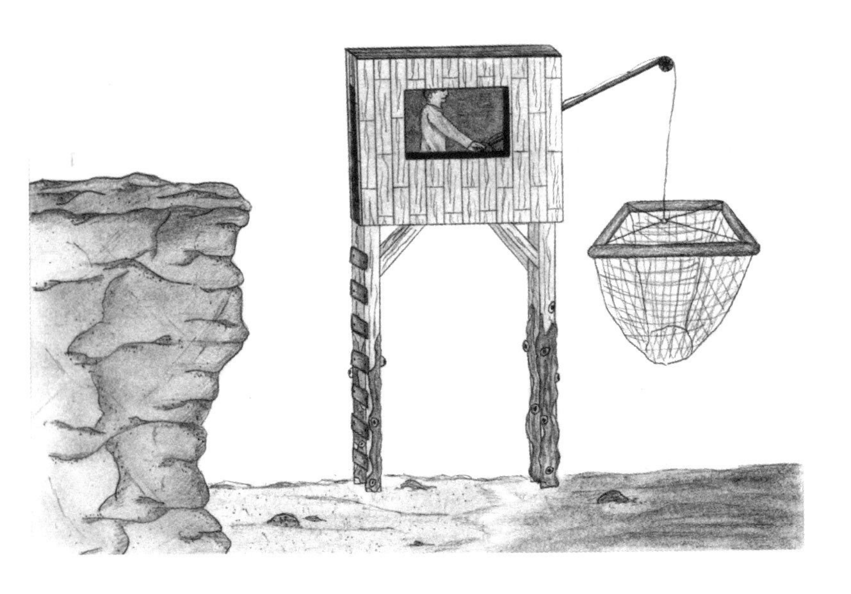

The Fishing Hut

# Fun and Games

Our American high school football team played teams from other American high schools in France; which meant we, our cheerleaders, teachers, chaperones and many others made frequent trips throughout France.

The soccer team also traveled; at that time the U.S. school sports system didn't include soccer and learning that sport well enough to make the team was something new and challenging.

Most of the time the games were so far away we had to stay overnight on base at  base military housing; usually close by their school or dorms.

Our school didn't seem to have the facilities to host home games; so ours was the fun of always getting to go other places.

It was a great opportunity to meet other overseas brats, to socialize, to party and to just have fun.

Earning those letters in sports was a big part of my life in France, and I wouldn't have wanted to miss that for anything.

# Who's That Again?

Our team was winning. We were really good. Well, the truth is; one guy was really good.

This player was so exceptional it was unreal.

He almost made a team by himself. One time he picked up a fumble, ran all the way down the field, made a touchdown without any help, and wasn't even breathing hard when we finally caught up with him.

I thought, "Wow, that's amazing! I've never seen anything like it!" We won almost every game and got to go to the playoffs. It was great!

It appears this is what happened:

When a family that had two boys, was about to be sent overseas to France, the brother who was in high school really didn't want to come. He wanted to stay at home with his grandmother and finish high school where he was.

Now, the other brother, a little older, was actually already out of high school, had started college and was playing college football. He very much wanted to be with his family, but he was too old to be an eligible dependent. So, the brothers traded identities.

No one even suspected until years later when the story finally was told.

# Dilemma

One afternoon we were late returning from an out of town game, and much to my dismay, I found I had missed my bus home. That was a problem.

I was hours away from home; I had no way to reach my parents, or anyone else.

There was no way to get home. There was no one around.

I knew no one was allowed to stay in the compound on weekends: there were no supervisors, the dorms were closed, and everyone had to leave; no exceptions.

I'd started walking around, trying to conjure up some sort of solution when I discovered I wasn't alone after all; another player was in the same predicament.

We put our heads together and still couldn't come up with anything. Slowly making our way around the compound, we dilatorily tried the dorm door.

To our surprise, it was unlocked.

There was power in two; we threw caution to the wind, put blankets over the windows for a blackout, and bunked down.

The long weekend eventually came to an end, no one discovered us, and we never told anyone.

# That's Not Lemonade!

The concern that officials had for dependents was never more apparent than in the colossal effort that was made to provide transport to school.

This wasn't easy because we were in a country that had just gone through a horrific war.

This was not a country dealing with business as usual; they were struggling with all their might to put their country back together again – to replace their roads and bridges – to get things back to normal.

To this end our troops were there to protect them from further invasion.

In order to do this, some of our parents were stationed away from base; their functions carried them throughout a large area of the country, and since this necessitated a long trip to school for some students, often ingenious ways had to be devised to get us to school.

A couple of times we had to ride the train on Sunday afternoon. Transport came to pick us up, but instead of taking us all the way to school, they gave us tickets and took us to the train station.

That was great fun. For one thing, in France there was no age restriction on liquor. They were selling those small bottles of liquor, along with pop and lemonade.

This was an opportunity not afforded in any other situation; and, of course, we took advantage of it.

As we emptied the bottles, we made a game of throwing them out the window at electrical poles along the tracks.

The great time ended, however, when at Rochefort, no one met us at the station, which meant we had to walk the mile or so to the base, carrying a couple suitcases each.

Now, this had been a several hour ride and many bottles had been thrown at the poles along the way.

Since early on I had decided I didn’t like the taste of liquor, I had the dubious advantage of being sober, and the thankless task of trying to encourage some of the others that had enjoyed a few too many that, “Yes”, they really did want to keep moving toward the base, and “Yes” we really did need to get to school.

# Please Salute

A few times we were transported to school and back in the general's car.

When we left the base, the driver and the guard were in the front seat. Then the other students got in and I got in last and sat in the back seat where the general usually sits.

I took the cover off the general's star with me as I walked by. When the cover was off the star, all military personnel had to salute as the car passed. When the cover was on the star it indicated the general was not in the car and they did not need to salute.

Now that I had the cover, everyone had to salute.

The driver and the guard didn't catch on right away, but it wasn't too long before they realized everyone was saluting as we passed.

They didn't know why; but eventually they must have realized what had happened. They stopped the car and told me to give them the cover. (I don't know why they figured it was me).

I gave it to them and they both got out. I was still sitting in the back seat of the car with the window down.

While they were out there, they started to talk to these French girls – and neither could understand the other.

The soldiers, of course, were speaking English and the French girls couldn't speak English worth anything; so they weren't doing too well.

I was laughing. Well, it *was* funny. At which point the military guy ordered, "You, get out here and translate."

Before, they were speaking very, very slowly, but once they thought they had a French translator, they were going a mile a minute.

I couldn't understand a thing they were saying; but, hey, I was in enough trouble already and I wasn't going to admit that so I just made it up as they went along; saying whatever I thought they wanted to hear.

When we left, they all had dates, and everyone was happy, especially me.

# Please Salute

# Deaf But Not Blind

One Sunday afternoon the transport came and it was a 2 ½ ton truck used to transport soldiers. We climbed in the back of the truck.

There were benches on each side and at the front. Now, these benches weren't padded benches; these were wooden benches – no give at all – and on these bad roads it was not exactly a soft ride.

But the worst part was that the two soldiers in front, the driver and the guard, told us that they went straight through.

This was a long ride and we usually had at least one stop; but the soldiers said we would stop for nothing.

That might have worked for soldiers; I'm sure it did, but high school boys, no way.

When nature called, we shouted and did everything we could to attract their attention. No luck, so, we just relieved ourselves out the back of the truck.

The guys in front either couldn't hear us or just ignored our shouts, but apparently they could see, because we only got that truck once!

# Combat Boots

Smitty never disciplined me, or yelled at me. There was one situation, though, that he did complain about, more than once.

It was about his shoes. Always on the move, I was not only rough on clothes; I was going through a pair of shoes a month. Getting home late Friday night and leaving again Sunday afternoon, left little time for shopping.

Now, the good news was that my feet were the same size as Smitty's . So when I left for school, I took a pair of his shoes and left my worn out shoes for him.

After this happened two or three times, as I was getting ready to leave one Sunday afternoon, all that was there to take was a pair of combat boots.

He grinned, "You won't wear those things out."

From the very first, when we arrived overseas, Smitty told me if ever I did anything wrong that required his superiors' attention, he would be called on the mat for it just as if he had done it.

I believe that all of the other kids had had similar warnings. Even though we got into pranks, if anyone ever got into serious trouble, the rest of us never knew about it.

I don't think that ever happened because we all knew the serious consequences it could bring.

# Beware

One day a reporter from a large U.S. newspaper came to interview the students at the American school.

Eager to talk with someone from home, we were happy to answer his questions about what we were doing, how we were getting along, our thoughts about school and other things.

Most of the students enjoyed talking with him and he stayed for quite a while.

It wasn't until the interview was over that he told us his newspaper didn't think kids should be there in France, and he'd been sent to get that story.

The article, of course, took the slant that children did not belong overseas in areas that had been torn by war.

The students very much disagreed with that point of view.

We wanted to be with our parents, and probably no student would have talked with him if we had known from the beginning what story he had come to get and that our words would be twisted to support that paper's position.

A lesson learned in being wary of reporters.

# Who? Me?

At bedtime, the lights went out. Well, they were supposed to go out but the dorm supervisor wasn't in our dorm so we covered the windows with blankets and, using French francs and centimes, sometimes played cards most of the night.

One night about midnight I was bored so I got another guy and some shaving cream and we headed over to the underclassmen's dorm. They were all asleep.

As I sprayed shaving cream on their hands, he tickled their noses; they immediately rubbed their faces, spreading the shaving cream all over, and woke them up.

After we had practically all of them awake, we went back to our dorm and I went to bed. They retaliated by storming our dorm, carrying pillows as weapons. I was the only one in bed as the pillow fight went on for some time, gaining momentum and noise as it went.

Eventually the supervisor came, walked right past all of those guys still pillow fighting clear back to my bed. He had been a marine.

I got to know him pretty well because I got blamed for everything that happened. (I heard later that for six weeks after I was gone, they were still blaming me until he finally told them to stop.)

His gaze drifted over me, "You're the one responsible for this and you are going to be the first one up in the morning. An hour earlier than normal here he came, pulled the covers off me, and opened the window to the cold France winter air. I had no choice but to get up.

# "Halt"

One day I was dropped off at the dentist office, off base at another military installation about six blocks away. When I was finished, I walked back to the base and up to the main guard house.

"Halt. Show identification." I didn't have any. We never left the base except on the bus or with a chaperone of some kind; family or school. There was never any reason for me to have identification.

The guard refused to allow me on the base. I could see the school but I couldn't get to it.

Here I was in a foreign country; my family was hours away without a phone, and these guys wouldn't allow me on the base. I couldn't persuade them, though I talked and talked.

Finally I asked, "What do I have to do, or what can I do, so you will let me in?" "You have to get some identification."

Exasperated, I came back, "Okay, how do I get that? I can't get on base."

He shook his head, "Well, you can try walking back over to the compound where you went to see the dentist and see if they can help you."

Still questioning I wanted to know, "How am I going to get on there if I can't get on here?"

He waved me off, "Oh, they'll let you on over there. They're not as strict as we are here."

So I walked those blocks back over there, and kept asking and asking until I finally got to the headquarters area. They said they could probably help me.

They sent me to an office where they took my picture, filled out a form (I don't know if they called the school or not) but they seemed to know what to do.

Anyhow, they made me an identification card and told me to go back to the school.

Then I walked those blocks back to the base.

This time I had identification. No problem. I showed the guard my identification, and finally walked in though that gate and the security of being back on base.

Now, when I came to think of it, that wasn't all bad. I could slip away anytime; now I'd have no problem getting in and out of the guard gates with my new identification card.

I explored the neighborhood, but found it wasn't very interesting. There was more to do on base so I didn't go off very often except that I did spend many interesting hours at the nearby ship museum which featured French battleships of WW1 and WW11, along with histories of past ships.

Though I didn't know it at the time, this was the ideal spot for a ship museum.

Those moats beside the school compound area had been used for shipbuilding for many, many years. The king of France had had his ships built there.

# Stash

We discovered that the tiles in our dorm ceiling could be shoved up and above them was space for all kinds of goodies; drinks, food, a bunch of stuff that was strictly off limits.

Over time we had accumulated quite a cache. From time to time we celebrated with a party. Then one weekend we came back to school to find we had been moved.

The girls were now housed in the boys' dorm and we had been moved to the girls' dorm.

We really didn't care except for our stash.

Now, the girls wouldn't give it back. They wouldn't even share. They claimed they couldn't find it.

We had no way to complain that they had kept our stuff – stuff we weren't supposed to have in the first place.

So, the girls won that one!

# Water Balloon

One evening during dorm study time I was quietly sitting there with my feet up on my desk when this guy came tearing in accusing me of having dropped a water balloon on him and his girl.

He was soaking wet and ready for a fight. They were standing beside the school when someone on the roof of the school, which was a three story building, had dropped a water balloon on them. They both got soaking wet.

I explained to him I had been sitting there reading the whole study time and asked him, "Did you come directly here after it happened?" He nodded, "Yes."

Then I reasoned, "If you came directly here, how could I have climbed down from the roof, run clear over here, already be sitting here and not even breathing hard?"

He admitted he didn't know, but added, "I don't know anyone else that would do that except you."

With that he took off trying to find out who had done it.

This was a very sad story. I sat there pondering how that could have happened – how could I not have known it was possible to get on that school roof?

# What Home?

On one particular Friday night our transport was a commissary bus, already crowded with ladies who had been shopping and their groceries were stacked up everywhere. We students crowded in and we headed out for the long trip home.

Finally they'd all been dropped off and all the groceries had been unloaded.

It was getting very late, about 10:30 or 11 pm.

Now we usually got home late, but always well before that hour. I was the last one on the bus as the driver explained, "We don't have an address to drop you off, and we have to get going."

Puzzled I questioned, "What about my usual address?" He shook his head, "Your family doesn't live there anymore. I don't know where they are, and I'm going to have to take you to the post and drop you off. I can't just leave you on the street."

When we got to the post, nothing new for me since we'd been there many times, he took me into the military police station and told them he had to go, and he had to leave me there because he didn't know what else to do with me.

The MP looked at me, "Well, we can't hold you here because you haven't done anything wrong; but you can stay here."

They didn't know where my family was, and they weren't able to find out, so they gave me something to eat and I settled in.

The night wore on, and still no word from anywhere. As it got later he decided, "You have to get some sleep. You can't stay up all night."

There was a small infirmary on the post; the only place there was for me to sleep, so he took me over there and told me to bed down for the night.

About 1:00 a.m. my parents showed up and said they were getting concerned, wondering why I didn't come home.

# French Draft

So we went home. As I discovered, home was really a hotel, where we were being housed temporarily just waiting for our paperwork to be completed, orders to leave France and return to the states.

We had heard horror stories of American teens being drafted into the French military, which apparently were true, because now the military was moving with unexpected speed to get military families with older teen boys out of the country.

We were all scheduled to fly back to the states together.

After all, I must admit kudos are due the griping corporal who was looking for 'Dudley Smith'.

But for his diligence, chances are Smitty wouldn't have been transferred out with the other men with older teenage boys, and possibly I would have ended up being drafted into the French army.

All of these families were gathered at the airport, ready, and the plane was on the runway, waiting but French customs would not let us leave.

They insisted our passports were not in order, this and that, you name it.

There were two MPs with the group, as well as the officer in charge, who finally got so disgusted he ordered the MPs to go over and secure the emergency exit. He then ordered the families to rapidly move through that door and quickly board the plane.

The plane immediately took off and we were headed back to the states.

CHAPTER SIX

# Home Again

It was not as if I'd just left yesterday. Not at all!

I had somehow expected things to stay the same while I was gone, and of course they hadn't. The songs were different. The way people dressed was different. Girls were wearing very full dresses like square dancers' skirts now. Lots of things had changed.

I didn't blend in very well. I have heard this over and over again from other overseas brats. It seems to be the norm. We had been introduced to different cultures, different ways of life, and different ways of thinking.

I believe we appreciated our government more. We discovered that other governments could fall, and the next day or two there would be a different government. We appreciated the stability of our government.

We'd had the opportunity to be ambassadors for our country; and I believe we'd been good ones.

I found cheating had increased. I also found bullying had increased and didn't intend to tolerate that.

In one class, there was a guy who was a real bully. He was a top student; football player, big, and loud. One day when the teacher left the room (I think that teacher was also the coach) he left this guy in charge.

He started to pick on a kid that was small, short, thin, and scared. He was hitting him, actually he was beating him. He was really on top of the little kid.

I stood up. He came charging toward me. I warned him, "You better make sure you know what you're doing because if you don't stop, this will be one sad day for you." He stopped about ten feet away. We stood and stared at each other.

Then he went back to the front of the room. When the teacher returned, the guy told him I was being disorderly. Irritated, the teacher walked back to me. I faced him grimly.

"The guy was pounding on that kid and I suggested he pick on someone his own size." "Don't let it happen again," he ordered. I didn't respond.

Then an exciting thing happened!

I met a kid who had at one point also been an overseas brat in France. Both of us were new to the school and we became good friends. At times, just for the fun of it, we would talk together in French.

One day a teacher came by and heard us speaking French. He questioned us, and when he discovered our backgrounds, he asked us to come and talk to his class. That opened up a whole new opportunity for us.

After that, many times we were asked to speak to classes. The kids weren't so different after all. They were interested in where we had been and our experiences overseas.

They had many questions—what were people like? the foods? the clothes? We told them it had been a learning time; and also a happy and fun time.

There was a lot of apprehension among the seniors. For most of them planning to go to college this would be the first time away from home.

For me, with 27 moves to my credit, it was just off for one more adventure.

It finally came to the end of the senior year, with graduation at hand. Then one of the counselors called me in and said I would not be able to graduate.

Though I had plenty of credits, way more than I needed thanks to the repeat year in France, they argued they could not give me a diploma because I had not had Florida history, nor did I have enough credits in physical education.

They considered irrelevant the fact that I had been on the football, soccer, and baseball teams in France.

Déjà vu. This couldn't be happening to me twice!

Fortunately, the admissions office at college held a much less exalted view of Florida history than Florida did, and I was off to college. I made it. College here I come—prepare.

I was no longer an Overseas Brat!

CHAPTER SEVEN

# Together Again

## Exciting Phone Call

A phone call which was out of the ordinary had my daughter, Elizabeth, puzzled. When I came home that evening, she told me someone had called wanting to know if her father had lived in France at one time. She told him, “Yes.” Did he go to school there?” “Yes, again.”

When she answered, “Yes,” she heard him excitedly announcing to someone in the background, “I found one. It’s him.” The questioning continued, “Was it in Rochefort?” That she couldn’t answer, but she did know it was in France.

I was elated, thinking, “It has to be some friend from Rochefort days.” All of a sudden, memories of those days came flooding back.

I soon discovered former students, calling themselves *Overseas Brats* had formed an organization and were searching for alumni of American overseas schools.

Already hundreds of us had been found. Meetings were being held all around the United States; the process was on a roll, and excitement ran high.

The next Overseas Brats national meeting was to be held in Dallas, and eagerly, I immediately made plans to attend.

I am an Overseas Brat!

# Overseas Brats Reunion

With great anticipation, I arrived at the reunion Until now I had not known such an organization even existed, and had no idea what to expect.

That Overseas Brats reunion was to me, amazing; something I'd never before experienced. I had, of course, been to other reunions where it was nice to see each other and catch up a bit; but there the resemblance ended.

This was like being reunited with family. I hadn't expected the emotional impact it had on me.

I discovered that Rochefort High School has its own alumni association (as do many other overseas American high schools) which has its own reunions every two years, as well as joining Overseas Brats for these combined reunions.

Because of the clever forethought of the meeting organizers, we were given lapel pins with our high school pictures on them, making it easy to recognize each other, as well as teachers and other staff members who attended the reunion.

There was a closeness rarely developed in any other situation, even living in dorms here in the states.

Somehow, because we were in a foreign country, far from home, some of us isolated on a base surrounded with a barbed wire fence, often even some distance from our own families there in France, with the constant knowledge of possible danger, this relationship was different.

At the reunion, now back together that closeness returned. The connection that we had had was immediately re-established – it was like yesterday.

We were almost like siblings, caring for each other, squabbling with each other.

I hadn't expected that. It surprised me. And it touched me.

The meeting was organized so that we had a lot of time to spend with our own Rochefort friends, and yet a good deal of time was allotted to spending with the overall group from all the schools.

The stories were endless. Mostly we rehashed many of the things that had happened in France, but other times experiences were revealed that previously hadn't been told.

What amazed me was to be able to sit down with any person that had attended any of the schools in any country and find our experiences so similar.

Each time we moved, we faced a whole new set of circumstances and were exposed to many totally different situations.

Learning to deal with them, I believe, gave us confidence to roll with the punches, to walk into any room of strangers and be confident that soon some of those strangers would be our friends.

One person claimed that being an overseas brat had been the most exciting time of his life, and I think we would agree that it was a significant time in all of our lives.

A clearer picture began to develop of why we had been in France.

As a student, I didn't know much beyond that we were there to protect the French people while they rebuilt. At home, Smitty didn't talk about his work. We discussed what the situation had been in France at the time, America's role there, and what our parents had actually been doing while we were there in France.

I gained a much more in depth knowledge of what had taken place. Now suddenly, I was looking back, no longer from a kid's view, but with an adult's view and with information to fill in a lot of gaps; wrapping up loose ends, pulling all those threads together.

There was too little time, too much catching up to do. As I left, I could hardly wait for the next reunion. And each reunion I attend leaves me eagerly anticipating the next one.

Overseas Brats is an organization and magazine for those associated with American Overseas schools, designed to serve the needs of thousands of "Overseas Brats." www.overseasbrats.com

Overseas Brats serves as a central reference point for those associated with overseas schools and provides them information on how to find friends and classmates, and assists where possible.

Actively seeking everyone associated with overseas schools since 1986, they have found more than 20,000 people. They help more than 240 overseas alumni groups representing 178 schools in 56 countries with their alumni organizations and reunion activities.

It creates opportunities for this unique group of Americans to meet and share our special heritage by renewing old friendships and making new friends at runions and Overseas Brats functions.

*Logo used with permission by Overseas Brats*

# Rochefort, France American High School Alumni Association

Rochefort, France American High School was in existence from 1953 to 1958, attended by not only Overseas Brats, but also by other Americans whose parents were in France for other than military reasons. Membership in the alumni association is open to anyone who attended as a student, served on the faculty, dorm supervisor or staff.

www.rochefortfranceahs.org

# The American Overseas Schools Historical Society

It was 2001; excitement ran high as hundreds of Overseas Brats converged on Wichita, Kansas for the AOSHS ground-breaking.

No one wanted to miss this moment in time. The story of overseas brats; memorabilia and memories that make up this unique part of history, would be collected and put on display.

We overseas brats and our families, as well as all Americans and others would now have the opportunity to visit this one- of-a- kind museum.

AOSHS, is the only organization in the world dedicated to collecting and preserving the artifacts and the history of American overseas schools, and to telling the story of educating an estimated 4 million American children, kindergarten through grade 12. 900 American overseas schools over the past 150 years.

The AOSHS office and archives are located in Wichita Kansas. It is possible to visit the Archives in Wichita to view the memorabilia collections or to do research.

Items from the AOSHS Archives are currently on display in the Museum of World Treasures (Wichita). The display changes every six months. Additional memorabilia arrives weekly, full of photos school records, trophies, awards, news clippings, yearbooks, pennants, class rings, written and video-taped histories.

For information about visiting the archives, making donations, or adding memorabilia to the collection: www.aoshs.org or

AOSHS Archives, 704 W. Douglas Ave., Wichita, KS 67203

# Appreciation

My appreciation, and admiration to those of you who started these organizations, built a data base of alumni, publish a magazine, and organize these meetings to provide opportunities for Overseas Brats to meet and keep in touch. Thank you.

# Family Reunited

It was while I was in college that the desire to meet and get to know my biological father became increasingly insistent; along with the hope that maybe he would want to see me.

With not a few misgivings, over holiday vacation, I plucked up my courage, found his address, and went to his home. Joe Lee did want to see me. He had always wanted to see me. He had heartbrokenly acquiesced to mother's belief that a child should not be pulled in two directions. He found it very hard; especially during the holidays, but he wanted what was best for me.

Joe Lee was a wonderful, loving man; and I was amazed, since I hadn't been with him, how my mannerisms, interests and enjoyments so closely echoed his.

If it had not been for the generosity and the caring, nurturing spirit of his wife, Tina, it would have been impossible for me to be enfolded into the family as I was.

Welcomed and accepted by my siblings, Ernest, Peggy, Mary June and Larry Joe, I became part of their lives and they became part of mine.

Though I'm very happy for the years we did share, still at his funeral, I could not stem the tide of tears - not only for his passing but for the precious years of his life I had missed.

It has been a major joy to be reunited with my family, and I thank God for this wonderful blessing.

*Other overseas brats share their memories*

---

DWA

Hi. My name is Brian and I'm an addict. I've been severely addicted for over fifty-three years. My drug of choice . . . Doo-Wop Music. I got hooked in 1955, while attending a high school for military dependants in Rochefort, France. Logistics of home and school prohibited a daily trip to and from school. This situation required me to reside in a dormitory on school grounds. Both male and female dorms housed students facing the same predicament. We were all children of U.S. servicemen stationed overseas. We went home on Fridays after classes and returned to school on Sunday evenings to settle in and prepare for the upcoming school week. The same scenario repeated itself for two and one half years. By then, my life was totally taken prisoner by Doo-Wop and rock and roll. How did I let it take over my soul? It was easy. I gave it away.

Living in a foreign country at the age of fourteen, away from family, and experiencing a new culture and environment, can be traumatic. Students living close enough to school were bussed in daily and went home every afternoon.

They ate home cooked meals, shared in family activities and had their own rooms to be alone, if need be. Not so, dorm students.

We slept in partitioned cubicles, four to a cube, with an aisle running the full length of the building. Cubicles weren't conducive to privacy or silence for studying and homework. We ate our meals in the Post cafeteria located about a quarter of a mile from the dorms. Snow and rain were not obstacles, if you wanted to eat. The Post Theatre, next to the cafeteria, was a source of entertainment for dorm students, but only on Wednesday and Sunday evenings.

Dorm students had to cope with loneliness, sickness and family separation by connecting with other students experiencing the same circumstances. An important part of a teenager's life is music. French music was not filling the void. We required our own music . . .from "home", meaning the United States. Fifties Doo-Wop and rock and roll were beginning to establish their own history. Slowly, the phenomena made its way across the Atlantic to overseas military institutions. Our music was gobbled up by lonely, hungry teenagers, namely dorm students.

The main, and extremely important gathering place was our recreation hall behind the dorms. Nightly, after study hall, everyone gathered to talk, unwind and catch up on the latest tunes to arrive from the U.S. We gravitated to the music and artists as if they were our only link to the outside world. It pulled us over and through many rough spots.

"AIN"T THAT A SHAME" when music allows you to "ROCK AROUND THE CLOCK" to keep your sanity? You sometimes feel that it's "ONLY YOU" carrying around "SIXTEEN TONS" of despair, but find later in life that "MEMORIES ARE MADE OF THIS" . You eventually close "THE GREEN DOOR" of your room at the "HEARTBREAK HOTEL" and give up "SINGING THE BLUES".

If you find yourself down and depressed, cuddle with your "EARTH ANGEL" over on "BLUEBERRY HILL" . . .go down to the seashore at "TWILIGHT TIME" and write "LOVE LETTERS IN THE SAND" or take a "SEA CRUISE" on the "SEA OF LOVE". Just don't get "ALL SHOOK UP". "CHANCES ARE" you'll find the "LOVE IS A MANY SPLENDORED THING" . Although "IT'S ONLY MAKE BELIEVE" reach for a "LITTLE STAR" and realize "ITS ALL IN THE GAME" of love.

Doo-Wop and rock and roll have possessed my life and soul. I gave up just listening to them. They've entered my blood stream and I've professionally sung their praises and lyrics for over fifty years. It's the first and only time that a pastime has completely changed my life. To me Doo-Wop is "A BIG HUNK OF LOVE".

By Brian R. Hulse

## WHAT I REMEMBER MOST ABOUT ROCHEFORT AMERICAN HIGH SCHOOL

We arrived in France, January 1955. I was a sophomore in high school. I discovered I would be going away to school on Sundays and returning on Fridays. The first part of the trip was by military ambulance. As I recall there were 3 students. We transferred to a military bus in Bordeaux (where we met a few more students) and were transported to Rochefort American High School, Rochefort, France. I remember my first impression of the school was . . .WOW. It had the appearance of a "high security" jail for juvenile delinquents. I, however, quickly fell in love with the place and it became a beautiful home away from home. I rapidly grew up and learned to be more independent. RESPECT, DUTY and RESPONSIBILITY were the cornerstones of our life in Rochefort.

As the end of the school year was approaching in 1955, I was honored to have been chosen as one of two students to represent our school at a week long summer Junior Red Cross Conference in Frankfurt, Germany. Students came from France, Germany, England and the USA. What a marvelous experience. We worked and played hard. Upon returning to Rochefort, it was my duty to start a Junior Red Cross chapter for our school. We did it! It would have been easier if the other student had been able to participate. As I recall, Trini Marble or Shirley Councilman was to be the second student and both were unable to participate. Much to my chagrin! It was a long trip for a 16 year old to travel alone.

Two interesting things happened on my way by train from Bordeaux to Frankfurt. I had to make a transfer in Paris a pretty big city for a small town boy like me from Kannapolis, North Carolina). I was directed by a U.S. military attaché to the correct track and train. I went aboard and shortly thereafter the train started to depart. One little problem, French trains are very prompt and this one was leaving 20 minutes earlier than my train. There was no porter to be found, so I did what anyone would do. Right! I pulled the emergency cord and several porters appeared immediately. I asked, where were they, when I needed them? They quickly turned me over to the military police. Again I was interrogated, but they concluded I had no choice but to react as I did and they escorted me to the correct train. I had a sleeper from Paris to Frankfurt, but it was shared with a young U.S. Army recruit He was only a couple years my senior. He took the upper bunk. During the night I heard a loud crash. The young man had a nightmare and accidently kicked the side window out in our compartment. Immediately we were surrounded by some upset French porters. In English they kept saying "You pay! You pay!" Fortunately the soldier admitted to the accident and they took him away. I proceeded on to Frankfurt without incident . . . but a lot wiser.

Other than the Frankfurt experience, my life at Rochefort was surreal. I loved the school, the teachers, our sports teams, the travel, the dorm, my fellow students . . .virtually everything. Recently, many of us met again after 50+ years at a high school reunion in Pinehurst, NC—October 28 - November 1, 2009. Among other things, we watched a 2.5 hour DVD of life at Rochefort in the "50's". We all agreed that it was a wonderful time in our lives and we will always look back with fond memories. Now that we have a DVD . . .that life experience has been resurrected and is available for instant viewing for the rest of our days.

Roney D. Raines Class of 57

# Special Thanks
# To

Pat Riley Blackwell
*Rochefort Alumni. www.rochefortfranceahs.org*

Ron D.. Raines

Brian R. Hulse

Joe Condrill
*Overseas Brats www.joeosbpres@sbcglobal.net*

Bobby and Shirley Rich

Megan Burkett

Sherry Davis

*The picture of the arch on the back cover was used with permission from the Kyrios family. Al Kyrios was the first principal at Rochefort American High School.*

# Return to France

Normally, the bi-annual meeting of the Rochefort Alumni Association is held in various locations within the United States, but one year the decision was made to return to Rochefort, France for the reunion.

It was a moving experience to visit the area where Rochefort American High School had once been.

Much had changed: the base was gone, the Quonset dorm buildings were gone, but the French building that had been our school was still there. It had been there for hundreds of years and will likely be there hundreds of years more.

Many of us traveled to the outlying towns where we had lived, distances that had required those long bus rides; noting with happiness that the cities and countryside had been restored , and were once again the beautiful country of France.

We were welcomed by city officials.

The American flag flew over the entrance to the area as a welcome for us the entire time we were there.

Many alumni took gifts from our governing officials to the Rochefort mayor; I carried greetings from our governor, as well as artifacts of the early French settlers in our state, and, of course, Green Bay Packers memorabilia.

One evening, when the meeting was over, and the official ceremonies were ended, an older lady stood and asked to speak. She merely said, "Thank you for coming."

We all knew she did not mean thank you for coming to-night – she meant, "Thank you America for coming when we needed you."

For me, it was the most poignant moment of the entire trip.

## Attending the Reunion in France in 1998

### Class of '54

Jerry Keltner and spouse Sharon
Margaret Ross
Dolores Harris Pair
Wayne "Sandy" Elliott and spouse Doll

### Class of '55

Ivory Herd and spouse Erma, plus 2 friends

### Class of '56

Irene Manley Ham and daughter
Shirley Counselman
Ginny Perez Torchia and spouse Tony
Billie Miller Phillips
Pat Riley Blackwell and spouse "Poor" Woody
Slim Milanoski and spouse Annette

### Class of '57

Maxine Zimmerman Knight-Otto and spouse Lou
David Friday and spouse Nicole
Arthur Bahme and spouse Myra
Bill Ross and spouse Louise
Kim Elliott Ashley

### Class of '58

Dudley Pippin and spouse Sue
Jerry Collier and spouse
Bobby Rich
Charlotte Lantz Kovalenko
Wynn Pope and spouse Carol
Faith Harris Rankin

### Class of '60

Lois Bohn McMullen and spouse Michael

# The Wedding

*This story is very special because the girl at the fence was Shirley, and the boy who suddenly had to leave was Bobby.*
*It is reprinted from "The Star", Port St. Joe, Feb. 13, 2003, with permission of the author, Tom Croft*

Every Day is Valentine's Day

You can see it in the eyes. Sit for a spell in the St. Joe Beach home of Bobby and Shirley Rich and the connection, that bond found in two halves of the same whole, is evident.

It is there in a photo shrine to their lives in a back hallway. It is there in the requisite photo albums and handy newspaper clippings. It is found in the St. Christopher medal Bobby has worn around his neck since 1956, a present from Shirley.

It permeates a chat about their marriage, and the vagaries of fortune that have ruled their lives. It is there in the easy smiles, the sentences started by one and finished by the other. But mostly, that love, that passion that has carried them over oceans and decades, is found in the eyes. Eyes that soften as they weave a tale Ripley wouldn't believe. Eyes that warm, sometimes glisten, as they recount a story of often star-crossed lovers which Danielle Steele might find implausible.

The story begins in France in 1954, when Bobby, now 65, and Shirley, 64, were teenagers and so-called "children of the Cold War." Both were military brats. Bobby's daddy was in the U.S. Army. Shirley's was in the Air Force. Both were stationed in the Bordeaux region and Bobby and Shirley were enrolled in the American High School in Rochefort.

The school was small. Shirley's graduation class was about 12. But the circumstances forged lifelong friendships, bonds that remain steel-like almost 50 years later. "It was a great group of people", Bobby said. "There was a lot of camaraderie in that situation. We were kind of like our own support group. If one kid had a problem, we all had a problem."

While attending school each week—the school was 100 miles from where their parents were stationed—the students lived in dormitories. Huts, actually, sleeping on army cots. Shirley remembered that there were two toilets, one sink and one shower for about 20 girls. "It was a choreographed dance getting ready every morning." Shirley said. "You got to be real close".

Bobby and Shirley quickly became sweethearts. For Bobby, it was his first love; Shirley had had a couple of boyfriends, "but nothing like that." Those heady times lasted until Bobby turned 18 the following year and his father was transferred stateside. When he left France, Shirley gave him a St. Christopher's medal with a personal inscription. Bobby left, but he was already pondering a way to get back to France and his girl. "I figured if I got in the military . . .I could get back there," Bobby said. His father was in the army, so a typically red-blooded and rebellious teenager, he chose the Air Force.

The Air Force recruiter was at lunch when Bobby arrived, so Bobby went next door and joined the Navy. Living in Oklahoma at the time, Bobby wanted to get to the East Coast and closer to Europe and Shirley. With ready knowledge of military thinking he figured the quickest way to the East Coast was to say he wanted to go to the West Coast. "I said, send me to the West Coast," Bobby said, "and they did. They out-foxed me."

In 1956 he sailed with his unit around the tip of South America to Boston, not realizing that Shirley had returned to America and was herself, in Bean town. The two had corresponded by mail, but they were continents apart at times and the mail not always timely. Through a friend,

Bobby also soon learned that Shirley had a boyfriend. Not the case, Shirley related. Yes, she had gone out with a boy a few times but to base functions because her father required her to have an escort. Bobby only knew she seemed to have found someone else and here he was a world away. He made a pragmatic decision.

"He wrote me a Dear Jane letter", Shirley said. And with that it appeared whatever life they might have enjoyed together was erased.. Actually that letter was no more than the pause button. Fast forward to 1993. Shirley had married, borne three sons, and divorced. She was a registered nurse in Maryland, in regular touch with a few of the high school chums she made in France. Bobby was frequently on her mind. 'I never forgot him,," Shirley said, noting that her sons used to play with a sailor hat of Bobby's. "My kids knew who he was."

Bobby had also married. He and his wife raised two daughters. He was an engineer living in Columbus, GA, and as far as his high school mates were concerned had dropped from the map. But the St. Christopher medal was still around his neck. That year the "Overseas Brats Organization," a kind of alumni group for former military brats or kids from embassy families held a reunion. Shirley attended and was downright giddy when she returned home. "It was 40 years, and it was like it was yesterday," Shirley said. "It was amazing."

She thought about Bobby. Where was he? What is he doing? She did some searching, the internet proving a useful tool. Her network of friends and classmates tried to assist. She was hampered with inquiries in French because Bobby Rich translates to "wealthy policeman." She once got a tip that he was in Fayetteville, NC. She called every Rich in the directory. She inadvertently got one man twice. He saved her soul both times.

But still, no Bobby. In 1996, some 40 years since she last heard from Bobby, she learned of a man in Texas who specialized in finding former military folks and their families. Shirley paid him $35 and exactly seven days later he provided the works on Bobby; Social Security number, wife, kids, work. Even three neighbors. Most importantly he had Bobby's address and phone number.

"Of course I had to call him," Shirley said, recalling the thunderous pounding in her chest. Her guise would be an upcoming reunion of the military brats in Washington, D.C.

In the time it took the electrical current to travel the phone lines, four decades melted away. "I never answered the phone," Bobby recalled. "I lived with a wife and two daughters. I was at the kitchen table, and for some reason I picked it up that time. As soon as I heard her voice I knew who it was." It was a hesitant, largely formal conversation, Shirley said. She relayed the information about the reunion. Bobby offered vague, non-committal replies. She said she'd mail him the information and they hung up. But something told Bobby she would be calling right back and he went into a bedroom. Sure enough, Shirley rang back, asking for Bobby's permission to give his phone number to several of their classmates from France.

Weeks later, Bobby disembarked from a plane in Washington to be greeted by Shirley and two of their closest friends from France. "It was magical," Shirley said of the moment. The love that had once burned, then flickered and apparently died, raged again. "You're scared to death of it," Shirley said, "because this is the last thing you expected."

Before too much more time elapsed—proportionately the equivalent of an hour when compared to the 40 years they missed—Bobby had extricated himself from the marriage that had gone south and he and Shirley were inseparable. "We wasted 40 years," Shirley said. "We didn't want to waste another minute." Despite what age and gravity had done to their frames, they were acting like teenagers again, Bobby said with a mischievous chuckle. Which would be a fine place for the story to end. But Bobby and Shirley had at least one more spin on the merry-go-round to go.

In 1998, the military brats were holding their reunion in Rochefort, where Bobby and Shirley had attended high school so many years, so many detours ago. "Wouldn't it be neat if we got married there," Shirley remembers thinking. "We went to Rochefort for a reunion and we had a wedding." Not just a wedding. They say France is for lovers, and the French, when they heard Bobby and Shirley's story, were enamored. The mayor of Rochefort insisted that a formal wedding be held in the town's special hall for such occasions. The mayor got dandied up to be the presiding officer, complete with official sash. This was at the same time that Europe was getting a look at the movie *Saving Private Ryan.* Memories of the release of France from the iron grip of Nazi Germany ran high. And the town of Rochefort, including the press and paparazzi, put on their spats for the American couple. An honor guard wore World War II-era "MP" uniforms for the wedding. After a dinner, the wine flowed and French wedding cake was devoured.

The couple received presents from complete strangers, who then lined the streets as they paraded and sang songs through town in a World War II vintage jeep. "A lot of people would have paid $1 million for that wedding," Shirley said. "We didn't pay a dime," Bobby finished. "It was really, really . . ." Shirley said, her eyes swimming just a moment. "It was amazing." And it made all the papers evidenced by the clippings Shirley has saved.

A couple of years ago the two retired, or at least semi-retired, to St. Joe Beach and the area’s sun and weather. Shirley’s kids love Bobby like he was their father. Bobby’s daughters are making the adjustment. The couple travel and hit the links and enjoy a life long denied.

“Sometimes you wish to heck (they’d found each other again) sooner,” Bobby said. “But that’s not possible, so you can’t brood on it. You can’t change it, you can’t undo it. You just have to be thankful. No regrets.”

“We missed so many years, so much fun, we have to make up for it. It’s been great.”

# Hermione

In July, 1997, the Hermione-LaFayette association embarked for a tremendous challenge—the reconstruction of the Hermione frigate—the ship which allowed La Fayette to join the American insurgents in the struggle for their independence in 1780.

In March 21, 1780 the major general La Fayette boarded the Hermione. He landed in Boston after a 38 day crossing and met General Washington to announce the impending arrival of French reinforcements to fight alongside the American insurgents.

In January, 1779, back from America, where he had volunteered to serve the American cause, La Fayette tried his best to obtain the official support of France.

He managed to convince King Louis XVI and his general staff to offer military and financial assistance to the troops of General Washington.

Hermione in combat at Louisbourg 1781—Wikipedia

In 1778, in Rochefort's arsenal, the Hermione started to be built on a construction hold near the Corderie Royale. Rochefort, a new town of the 17th century was born to develop a new Royal arsenal on the banks of the Charente in order to construct, arm, supply and repair a war fleet able to resist enemies' assaults.

Now the Hermione is being reconstructed. The shipyard is in one of the two dry docks beside the Corderie Royale at Rochefort, a cavernous 18th century cobblestone dry dock. As far as possible, 200-year-old methods of boatbuilding—such as using iron chisels and hammers are used, although modern power tools were substituted for period tools on some jobs.

Plans include equipping the ship with modern navigational tools for the trip across the Atlantic. The site is open to the public and admission fees help fund the project. Visitors can get a close-up view of the process of piece by piece reconstruction of the 145-foot, 32-gun, three-masted frigate.

The Hermione will always be linked with helping the United States win its war of Independence and already flies the flags of both countries. The organizers promise to sail on Lafayette's route, perhaps with a joint French and American crew.

The event will be celebrated in the United States. An entire year of festivities are planned.

Additional information: www.hermione.com

---

*We are eagerly looking forward to the Hermione arriving on the East Coast. During our reunion in France we toured the construction site, the moat beside our Rochefort American High School*

# Two Brothers

The kid brother of Charles and Corbin, my uncle, James, died very young. leaving two boys, little more than babies. The grieving, distressed mother allowed family to help with the two little ones and eventually the little boys were separated, the mother with the younger one Charlie, and a family member with the older boy, Jimmy.

Each grew up never knowing of the existence of the other brother.

The mother moved out of the area, and all searches for Charlie proved fruitless. The family could only pray.

Then, out of the blue, a few months ago, James' sister Eloise received an unusual telephone call. Eloise thinking it was someone searching for his family, but not quite sure, used her cell phone to call my sister, Sherry and attempted to put the cell phone up to the land phone so Sherry could take the call. When this didn't work—they couldn't hear each other—she gave him Sherry's phone number.

Somehow, it was right at that moment I called Sherry. She quickly said, "I'm waiting for a phone call; I think it might be Charlie." With hope suddenly rising in me, I rapidly ended the call.

Then he called Sherry – and Sherry knew who he was – Charlie. He had found his family. And we had found him. What a happy phone call that was. He was excited! We were excited!

Charlie had done research. He had used his last name,

Harris, and had hit only dead ends; he could not find his family.

He had very little information but at some point in the past, he now remembered, he had heard the names Eloise and Jack – with the last name of Mc "something."

He was not sure what, but McDonald was one of the possibilities. For the last two or three years he had been calling every area code in Florida, following every possible lead.

By the greatest of blessings, he called when he did, for had he waited just two more weeks, that phone number would have been disconnected for Eloise was moving from her home and it would have been nearly impossible to reach her.

Now, he wanted to meet the family at Sherry's home in Florida. When he learned that I was due to come to Florida in a week or so, that I had known his father well, and we had lived together as children, he quickly made plans to come to meet the family at Sherry's home. In Florida, As many of the family as could at such short notice, planned to be there to meet him.

When I arrived there, Charlie was expected during the next day. Then he called. "I'm so excited I'm going to drive all night. I'll arrive early in the morning."

And he did. Before long, he drove in with his wife and baby. What a happy time!

He looked so very much like I remembered his father, James, when we were kids together at home.

---

*Jack McDonald 1929-2009*

Imagine his great excitement when he discovered he had a brother – a full brother – he knew nothing about – and his brother, Jimmy, knew nothing about him.

Now, Charlie was eager to meet his brother. Jim was contacted, and Sherry set up Skype so the brothers could talk with each other. They talked for four hours. It was an emotional time.

In wonder, Charlie said, "He looks so much like me, it's like looking in the mirror; except his shirt is different."

Of course they wanted to meet and actually see each other. All that was possible at that point, was a brief encounter as Jim went back to Kuwait.

Thoughts immediately went to a family reunion, but plans were not easy to schedule.

Jim was overseas. While we had always known Jim was our family Jim didn't always know we were his family, and we were eager for him not only to meet Charlie but also to be with us as family. The reunion would need to be scheduled when he was back in the states.

Eventually a date that would work was set and extended family excitedly made plans to attend the reunion.

My brother Mark, a retired Seabee, now returns as a civilian to do much the same service he did in the military. We have only a vague idea of the region where Mark may be at any given time, and an even more vague idea of what service he may be rendering.

By the greatest of luck he was on one of his quick visits home when Charlie visited. They were able to get acquainted, and as a result, before long Charlie, who had recently returned from Iraq, temporarily joined Mark overseas on his current project.

At last the waited reunion date was almost here. Mark and Charlie were ready to leave. Then at that very time, in that very place, the tragic international incident in Kabul occurred. For them to leave was out of the question. They could not get home for the reunion!

We wait with anticipation the day of the rescheduled reunion. It will happen.